BICYCLING
ACROSS
AMERICA
A JOURNAL ON THE OPEN ROAD

Do it!

David [signature]

12 April 2007

DAVID HESTON FENIMORE

PINEDROP PRESS
CRYSTAL BAY, NEVADA

ISBN 0-9621627-0-1

Library of Congress Catalog Card Number
88-92637

Printed in the United States of America

Pinedrop Press
P.O. Box 284
Crystal Bay, Nevada 89402

Thanks

To Mary-Carol Larson, Jr., for typing up the original scribblings;
to Barbara McDermott (Mac) for typesetting, paste-up,
cover photo and cover design;
to Maggie Graff for the title page illustration;
to Marty Cohen for use of Tahoe Crafts's facilities; and
to the estate of my maternal grandmother, Edith Raymond Heston,
for partial funding.

To our grandparents, who might have tried
something like this if they'd had the time.

And to my wife, Nanci Neva Northway,
who created this idea and nurtured it with love to its conclusion.

—DHF

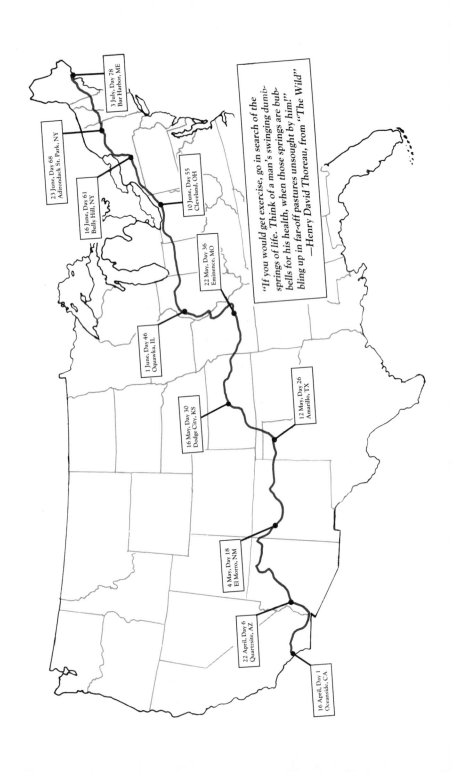

3 July, Day 78
Bar Harbor, ME

23 June, Day 68
Adirondack St. Park, NY

16 June, Day 61
Bully Hill, NY

10 June, Day 55
Cleveland, OH

22 May, Day 36
Eminence, MO

1 June, Day 46
Oquawka, IL

16 May, Day 30
Dodge City, KS

12 May, Day 26
Amarillo, TX

4 May, Day 18
El Morro, NM

22 April, Day 6
Quartzsite, AZ

16 April, Day 1
Oceanside, CA

"If you would get exercise, go in search of the
springs of life. Think of a man's swinging dumb-
bells for his health, when those springs are bub-
bling up in far-off pastures unsought by him!"
—Henry David Thoreau, from "The Wild"

The Statistics

Length of Tour .... 4657.7 miles

Start .... Oceanside, California; April 16th, 1986

Finish .... Bar Harbor, Maine; July 3rd, 1986

Average Daily Mileage 70

Approximate Load per Bicycle .... 45 lbs.
(not including machine or rider)

Ratio of Nights in Motels to Nights Camping 2:1

Flats 8

Rainfall .... every 2nd or 3rd day after Kansas

Most Common Roadside Scene .... cornfield

Significant Books Read During Tour ....
William Least Heat Moon, *Blue Highways*
Mark Twain, *Huckleberry Finn*

Most Recent Accomplishments. . . stayed married; kept careers on track

Favorite Foods .... raisins, graham crackers

Beverages of Choice .... polyethylene-flavored water; beer

Table of Contents

Foreword

There was this kid I used to know in grade school named Ward Abronski, and one day in the dining hall he told me we should get some of these special maps from the police department and ride our bicycles across the country. I thought he was crazy, but I never forgot his suggestion, and thirty years later I schemed and plotted with my wife Nanci and we finally did it.

What follows is a mass of mostly unrevised jottings transcribed from three tattered spiral-bound notebooks, scribbled during stolen moments in low-rent motels, on picnic tables in the rain, inside our windblown tent, or on the formica counters of smokey roadside cafes.

The numerous variations in tone, tense and style in these journals should be excused as reflections of our daily states of mind and of the endless parade of tenacious towns, empty fields, and suggestive horizons. We offer you this series of snapshots receding into the misty distance, a scrapbook of the changeable skies and straightforward faces along the asphalt trails of America.

> —David Heston Fenimore
> *April Fool's Day, 1989*

BICYCLING
ACROSS AMERICA
A JOURNAL ON THE OPEN ROAD

Chapter One:
The Pacific Southwest

April 16, 1986 Day 1
51.5 miles
Oceanside to Lake Henshaw, California

If we had to begin somewhere, I guess it would be with the night-before slumber party at Skip and Diana's apartment in La Mesa—the whole crew minus one plus four bicycles. Breakfast, the first of many versions across America, was at Hob Nob Hill in San Diego, where Julie joined us. Our table of seven included Matt and Paula who drove us down from North Lake Tahoe, where a foot of snow still surrounded our house. Then there was my wife Nanci, Randy, Julie's college roommate's husband Mike Aguirre, and me. The service at Hob was prompt and friendly—so were the fresh o.j. & blueberry pancakes—and Michael told us some of the local scuttlebutt: how the conservatives are beginning to back no-growth measures since they've seen the havoc uncontrolled development has wreaked on the town. But it may be too late for this coastal paradise.

Next stop was at Oceanside Beach, where we parked next to the sand (0 ft. above sea level) and swarmed over the bicycles for hours, loading them up, installing and testing equipment, balancing loads, distributing food, and finally lugging the loaded bikes to the edge of the water for the obligatory "before" photographs, filling the carefully-cleaned chains with sand. A policeman showed up to tell us we couldn't park there without a beach permit, so we took off—Nanci, Randy, Julie, and myself—with Matt & Paula shadowing us in the van for the first few blocks as we rode the wrong way south along the beach road. The

---

towering thunderheads out over the ocean failed to produce any weather, and once we turned around and left the coast, the sun and wind were with us the rest of the day.

For the first five miles out of town we were shoulder-to-shoulder with fuming buses and roaring trucks along Route 76 East. We stopped at Mission de San Luis Rey (1798), admiring the icons set in niches on the huge whitewashed walls and the skull and crossbones carved over the cemetery gate. Catholic rites are still celebrated here.

As our tailwind blew us up the winding San Luis Rey valley, through fragrant orange, lemon, and avocado groves, the road grew less travelled but remained in excellent repair. We stopped for lunch by a large geranium bush on the edge of a field being cultivated, and feasted on rolls from Shatz of Bishop, jalapeño cheese, Dijon mustard, and fresh strawberries we'd bought on the outskirts of town, at a little produce stand where a peacock strutted around outside.

A short climb, our first, led us through the Pala Indian reservation and down into the Pauma Valley. From there we climbed steeply for five miles up the slopes of Mt. Palomar to about 4000 feet—windy and cold but slanting golden rays over the hills. We suited up and descended rolling terrain another ten miles, the last few in the dark, to Lake Henshaw, where we camped among the recreational vehicles. Our legs were so sore we could only walk sideways, like crabs, to the heated restrooms.

April 17th   Day 2
47.6 miles
Lake Henshaw — Agua Caliente, California

Morning at Lake Henshaw (el. 2727 ft.) was partly cloudy, windy, and cool. After a hearty breakfast at the resort cafe, with a salty young woman entertaining us and the many sport fishermen ("What do you expect, coming in here smelling like fish?") and the San Diego paper and homemade salsa and free coffee refills, we pedalled along the lake, wearing our windbreakers against the coolness, through open fields of orange, yellow and purple flowers, and huge old oaks.

Passing the turnoff for Santa Ysabel Mission and a huge array of solar collectors, we hung a right on S-2 and began the reasonably shallow climb to Teofulio Summit (3636 ft.). From there a long, rolling descent past San Felipe, junction of the Great Southern Overland Stage Route of 1849 and old Dieguino Indian trading trails, past the small town of Vallecito, and thence into Anza-Borrego State Park, the nation's largest. Here are huge ocotillos, blooming red at the tips, purple flowers on stubby bladed cactus, cholla, and other low desert vegetation. The desert is perfect for riding now—not much traffic, a cool tailwind, and diminishing clouds. The air is still quite brisk, so I alternate tights and windjacket with shorts and t-shirt.

Anza-Borrego has a short climb; at the summit we lunch amid piles of brown rocks at a narrow pass overlooking the green desert basins. A descent to the Stagecoach Store and RV park for refreshments, then a short climb to a saddle overlooking the lower desert, from which an exhilarating steep descent with a long runout along the flats leads to Agua Caliente, a San Diego County Park. The mountains about us have lost any vestiges of vegetation—just dull bushes that blend into the rock walls. The Laguna Mountains furnish a very interesting ridgeline, in broad jagged relief against the clear blue sky. I understand there's a trail up there along the top of the towering wall. The air's clean and infinitely transparent. We can appreciate the tailwind by default on the occasions when the road jogs to one side or the other, causing our progress to be reduced considerably.

Somewhere near here there's a storytelling festival held late every spring in honor of Pegleg Smith, an early resident. One of his favorite tales concerns a feminine newcomer to the high desert northeast of here, holding her skirts down in a howling gale. "Does it blow this way all the time?" she asked an old desert rat, who replied, "Nope. Only half the year. The other half it blows the other way."

The rangers at Agua Caliente have some captive snakes and lizards they use for instructional purposes—a man and woman, young and pleasant (the rangers, not the lizards—the latter are kept in the refrigerator to slow them down). Camping is $7 for a tentsite. Two pools are open:

the outdoor swimming-style pool against the mountain slope, and the Indian pool, a hot springs-style rock tub. Both about 80-85 degrees. The huge indoor jacuzzi, artificially heated to 101 degrees F, closed at 3 p.m. so we missed it for today. The water from the campground taps is 70-75 degrees and smells faintly of sulphur. Tame bunnies scamper about, just out of reach, and the hooting, plaintive, yet rooster-like call of the white-winged dove haunts us. We camp in a secluded spot beneath overarching honey mesquite trees, scaring Julie with tales of scorpions and snakes.

I'm very proud of my homemade brake bar: a chip of wood from the pilings outside a produce stand in Oceanside. Wedged between the brake lever and brake housing, it locks the pads to the rims and parks the loaded touring bike securely. Jim Blackburn sells a plastic doodad with a leash to do the same thing for $2.60. I feel like this small improvisation has gone a long way toward setting a tone of simplicity for me at the start of the trip, until I lose the piece of wood and have to fish my Blackburn brake bar out of my tool bag. There's no end to the various devices that purport to make outdoor expeditions more efficient—case in point, my new digital cyclometer, with which I'm also quite impressed—but there is a point of diminishing returns.

Randy got up last night with the binoculars to look for Halley's Comet, but a temporary haze filled the sky at the appropriate viewing time. He's been busy charting the course of the waxing moon, sketching diagrams in his notebook for an astronomy class he's taking. He vows to set up a comet watch every evening during the remainder of his time with us.

April 19th   Day 3
52.8 miles
Agua Caliente — El Centro, California

Breezy this morning, but warmer, and nary a cloud to be seen. We're waiting to cap our pancake breakfast with a dip in the indoor pool, which is full of the obese elderly. It stinks to high heaven of chlorine. We all get in, but not for long. Soon we're rolling out of the park, down S-2, past the Fan Palm Canyon (California's only native palm, grows in these high hidden defiles where there's a steady water supply), and over a pretty good summit with a view over the Carrizo Badlands (and Impact Area, i.e., military gunnery range). Then more desert riding to Ocotillo, at Interstate 8, where we bought lunch at a grocery and ate it in the shade of a Bible church. While we were making sardine sandwiches, Randy's rear tire blew with a loud pop and hiss. He patched it, but it didn't hold, so he patched it again, and again, and finally had to use his spare tube.

Julie has gotten tired of wearing her helmet so she carries it strapped to her gear. Yesterday it apparently worked its way loose and rubbed against her tire, leaving huge black streaks and abrasions through to the foam liner, making it look like she took a horrible fall.

At Ocotillo we turned East along the Evan Hewes Highway, the old road to El Centro. It's kind of rough, paralleling the Interstate, but has hardly any traffic. For a while the desert predominates, and 12 miles south the brown mountains of Old Mexico beckon. We ride through Plaster City, site of a gypsum wallboard plant, and then from hot resinous desert we enter the cool, wet, manure-like atmosphere of irrigated alfalfa fields. We rode the 20-plus miles into El Centro in one long shot, and pulled into a Motel 6—$25.95 for four, showers, and a warm tropical walk in clean clothes through town to an excellent dinner at El Sombrero. A pitcher of beer ensured we wouldn't last very long after dinner.

April 20th Day 4
60.81 miles
El Centro — Chocolate Mountain Summit, California

El Centro is a stunning series of fast food strips, with all the usual southern California drive-in mania: low, flat, multi-colored structures of plastic and prestressed concrete. Breakfast at Brunner's, a high-volume basic coffee shop with good service and ho-hum food except for the country fries with onion and bell pepper.

We're girding up for the desert crossing—about 50 miles with no services, according to hearsay and the map. Extra water bottles, food, and sunscreen are the order of the day. It would have been nice to get riding by 6 a.m., when it was cool and windless, but we haven't learned our lessons in desert travel yet. Randy's tire repair, along with lunch, spontaneously kept us out of yesterday's midday heat. We may still get our earliest start yet today at 9 a.m. With a good tailwind (forecasts vary) we could make it almost to Blythe. The cool shelter of a long-sleeved white polypropylene shirt works well in this climate.

Chatty schoolmistress—pert, pixy-like, short-haired, driving a Blazer—pulled up to us when we first hit town yesterday. "I'm a jockette," she declared, and wanted to know everything about us. We actually found out more about her: she grew up in Utah and said she gladly traded snow shoveling for three months of 115 degrees.

Cyclotouring is like continually looking through a microscope: just as the biologist sees a whole world in a sample of ordinary pond water, so the bike tourist sees the riot of humanity and other roadside attractions in much greater detail than the motorist does. Places we wouldn't ever consider stopping at, places that look like forlorn shacks from the freeway, come alive to the bicyclist with their treasures of food, water, sodas, and local lore. Of course, traveling at 10 mph you don't usually have much of a choice.

The roads took us at alternate right angles out of El Centro, riding past all kinds of developing agricultural products. Just before Highway 78 cut off to Blythe, a cropdusting plane swooped around the powerlines, spraying some turnip fields, directed by a man in a yellow slicker suit. We could smell the chemicals. Off in the distance, the yellow-brown of the dune fields to the northeast was visible like a low ridge of polluted air on the shimmering horizon. Heading towards them, we came after a while to a corner store where we stopped for the morning snack at some shaded picnic tables out in front. One old desert rat drove up in his rattletrap pickup, leaving it running "to let the turbo cool." His portly Indian wife remained in the cab despite his invitation to "come on out 'n' stretch your legs." He'd once worked at the mines up the road somewhere, and now lived west of Blythe in Mesa Verde. Then another guy drove up in an RV, more cleancut and prosperous-looking than the first fellow, with a military visage and Op corduroy shorts. While chatting with us he made repeated runs into the store for Bud Lights. He bemoaned the BLM's having closed off one side of the dunes, where he said there was an interior valley full of wildflowers. He was an avid off-road vehicle enthusiast, and said, "Too bad you don't have time to get a ride on one." Then he bought us a big bag of the house's special chili peanuts (chili, garlic, touch of cayenne, salt).

Further up the road we came to a scene from Road Warrior Hell: hundreds of ATCs, dunebuggies, and a few motorcycles crawling over the smooth sand mountains of the Imperial Dunes, sending plumes of dust spewing into the breeze. The drivers and riders, some of them looking rather overweight, were heartily partying, their bellies jiggling with the bumps, beer coolers strapped to the rear racks on their vehicles. We climbed over two successive low summits with all this activity snarling on our right; to our left, only desert vegetation bloomed among the legally off-limits sand hills, and the Chocolate Mountains beyond looked evermore chunky and chocolatey in the lowering sun. Is this Candyland?

At Glamis, where Skip and Diana had warned us not to expect water, we found ATC Central, "The Beach Club," a pizza joint and beer hall with dozens of motorized trikes snarling in the parking lot. Julie ventured inside to clean her contact lenses, and reported numerous offers of a sexist nature along with a warning not to drink the tap water, said to be "full of arsenic and salt." Water was definitely not the beverage of choice with this crowd, whereas two of us had plastic gallon jugs of the precious fluid precariously tied to our panniers.

While Julie researched the locals, the rest of us took refuge in the shade of a few old wooden storage sheds by the Southern Pacific tracks that crossed the road a little further on. We laid out our lunch in the gravel, and then just as we began an old fellow drove up in front of us, to check, he said, if we were the one out of a hundred that would vandalize the railroad buildings. Seeing we were harmless, he stayed to talk, mentioning other bicyclists who'd passed through, from collegiate groups of a hundred with buses and pilot cars, to the lone woman in the dead of the 115-degree summer, whom he mercifully ferried to Palo Verde.

"Seen any wets?" he grinned. "Illegals. They mostly follow the railroad tracks; river's too rugged. 20,000 a month are caught by each of three border patrol units. Just a numbers game, 'cause they all come right back in—all they do is drop 'em across the border."

No sooner had he left than a freight came roaring by, and in its wake we saw two men, dark-haired and shirted in shiny black polyester, one with a shoulder bag, the other with a paper bag, following the tracks northwest through the sandy desert. Did they jump from the speeding train? It would be a long, hot walk to anywhere.

As we packed up to leave we discovered that Randy and Julie's water jugs had leaked, filling their panniers and soaking their clothes and sleeping bags. So we poured most of the remaining contents into our water bottles, drank the rest, and biked on through the afternoon heat along the Ben Hulse Highway.

Hulse, we learned from a roadside pylon, was a "civic-minded citizen" and senator who championed construction of the road to Blythe, completed in 1964.

The Mesquite Mine guarded the low summit over the Chocolates—a prosperous-looking operation with brand-new banjo-wired cyclone fencing and freshly painted sheet metal buildings linked by over-the-road conveyors. Dry camp tonight, with a bright half-moon. The marker near where we went off the road to camp, and one at the crossing of the Chocolates, explained that Route 78 follows an ancient Indian trail from the Palo Verde Valley/Colorado River to prehistoric Lake Coachella, now the dried-up and irrigated Imperial Valley.

The lack of surplus water worried me in camp, but we cooked rice and veggies and ended up with extra. Randy is of the opinion that rationing water does no good—better to drink freely and run out than take occasional small sips. Fortunately we did not have to test his hypothesis. The little bit of water someone has left over from Agua Caliente tastes terrible, even with lemonade mix.

April 21st   Day 5
68 miles
Chocolate Mt. Summit, California — Quartzsite, Arizona

Sunday morning was our earliest start yet, 7 a.m., and though it was already warm, the residual coolness was nice. After some dips in and out of washes, the road took a long curving descent through the Chocolate foothills into the Colorado River basin, past flowering desert trees and unpaved turnoffs on the right to river campgrounds. As the terrain flattened, the canals and emerald-green irrigated fields, many with harvested haybales still scattered, began to closely resemble those of the Imperial Valley. As we passed the Cibola Wildlife Refuge the flocks of birds became more numerous.

We breakfasted at the only cafe in Palo Verde, on friendly food with choices of pinto beans or crisp cottage fries, cornbread (they were out), or hamburger patties. We washed up, sunscreened, redressed, stocked up on water and snacks, and rolled through more fields another 20-plus miles to an I-10 overpass, then east along the frontage road to Blythe, another ever-increasing strip of fast food, auto parts, and shopping malls. Much of it was closed. The heat of the day mounting, Randy and I went in search of a bike shop to get an extra water bottle and a 26 x 2.125″ tube for his mountain bike tire, but found none in the few open shops. Julie and Nanci went shopping for lunch, and we all met at a riverside RV park, a lawn-like setting just south of the I-10 bridge over the Colorado, with shade trees, jet skis, and many Americans in full camping regalia. It cost us $4 but was worth it for a siesta on what feels like the hottest day yet.

I can't help admiring the new season's bathing suits, but while trying to snooze we're forced to overhear the couple next door having it out: the young fellow in cutoff jeans, wallet chained to his belt, is foully cursing his female companion. Her replies are inaudible, but it's got something to do with getting the tent up. Even now it continues, as he comments on the size and odor of her posterior, with liberal use of the "f-word." Is this what comes of being confined inside a car in this heat?

After lunch and siesta we crossed the Colorado River and rode the interstate for 20 miles to Quartzsite. A long gradual climb—and our first saguaro cacti—followed by a long exhilarating descent, about 10 miles at 20 mph into Quartzsite. The freeway shoulder is perforated every 20 feet or so with bar-like depressions, meant to jolt dozing drivers. We call them the "de-dump de-dumps." They are a slight annoyance, which we can avoid by riding on the white line between the shoulder and the right lane when there's no traffic. Randy just plows through the gravel on his fat tires.

Julie and I speculate on whether we're going to stay at the Holiday Inn or the Rodeway Inn in Quartzsite, discussing the comparative merits of each as we roll down the off-ramp, but Quartzsite is a bit smaller than expected so we settle for the Stagecoach, a "25 hours/day" motel/restaurant asking $27.50 for a small room with two large beds and a color TV. Our hosts: Bud and Bernice. We drink a six-pack of Corona during showers and watch *Superman III*. Julie is so hard up for a shower (and glad, probably, that we're not sleeping with the spiders and snakes again) that she calls this slimy place "the best motel I've ever stayed in."

April 22nd   Day 6
95 miles
Quartzsite — Wickenburg, Arizona

> Mankind is like squadrons of bicycles running amok. We should every one fall off if we didn't ride so thick that we hold each other up.
>
> —D. H. Lawrence, *Fantasia of the Unconscious*

Today is John Muir's birthday. We didn't get much of a desert start: 8 a.m. MST. Ten more miles of Interstate 10, then off on State Highway 60 East for a long pull through desert basins and tiny dilapidated towns like Hope, which is for sale. Very hot—the thermometer at the grocery in Salome (where we bought Tastycakes and other staples) read 99 degrees in the shade. Randy has a slightly desperate air about him as he packs down the peanut butter.

Mark Twain tells a story about a cavalryman near Yuma who died of the heat one Arizona summer, went to hell and immediately sent back for his overcoat. As we sit on the grocery store's porch, eating and drinking, a leathery old guy comes out the door, clutching a frosty six-pack of Coors Light as he swings up into his pickup. "Hot?" he asks rhetorically. "Hell, this is just right!"

Salome owes its existence to Dick Wick (-enburg) Hall, turn-of-the-century editor of the *Wickenburg Times-Herald*, who founded Salome

("Where She Danced" is the town motto) and irregularly published a mimeographed sheet of wit and lies, his most famous feature being the frog who was seven years old and hadn't learned to swim.

> Out in the desert is where I sit
> Just trying to get used to it.
> All the water I've got to drink
> Is what leaks out of the kitchen sink.
> We don't need the law to keep us dry
> Even the clouds just pass us by.
> I was set down in the sand here by mistake
> 300 miles from the nearest lake.

Representations of the frog, and a dancing stick figure with a veil, adorn some of the town's buildings. Many older people around, and plenty of RV's and mobile homes; I think the retirees must come here to escape the high pollen counts in Phoenix and Tucson. Also some farming—fruit & nut trees, alfalfa—and the Central Arizona Project canal which runs perpendicular to our route.

Someone wrote that bicycle tourists are obsessed by two things: the weather and the condition of their machines. Right now, long-sleeved white turtlenecks and Number 15 sunscreen are very important to me. The low humidity helps too, especially when we're moving, evaporating that sweat. Never so hot as when we stop.

But it's slow going climbing out of this basin, up to the plateau on which are Salome and the Mountain Pass Cafe, where two telepathic old women—sisters perhaps—served us cold drinks. The heat is debilitating. In fact, this part of the route presents serious psychological obstacles to survival. It *looks* hot. There's a tale told hereabout of a New Yorker who arrived at the Tucson railway station in August. His blue serge suit got off the train, but the Easterner had evaporated.

However, this is April, the afternoons cool off nicely, and there's some great bicycling terrain from here to the end of the day: flat, with ever-so-slight upgrades or downgrades, wide shoulders, and yes, a slight tailwind. It's surprising that, from a few hundred feet of elevation at the Colorado River, we've climbed to over 2000 feet at Salome and Wickenburg, with a nearly imperceptible 1000-foot climb between the two towns; we were hitting long stretches of 20 mph between Salome and Aguila, and stretches of 13 mph on the climbs. It felt good to keep a 60-70/minute cadence for 10-15 miles at a time.

Something about Aguila none of us liked: it could have been the preponderance of sullen citizens drinking beer in the street, or lounging in front of the markets and liquor stores, but nobody liked the 15-20 minutes we spent there, drinking sodas in front of the liquor store in which an enormously fat man, shirt hanging open and his exposed skin blotched by something like "haole rot," stood drinking beer and talking to the skinny, squinting owner.

One routine that has developed is filling our water bottles with the gallons of spring water we buy for a dollar each at the small markets; tap water hereabout is pretty awful, but, of course, we have been totally spoiled by Tahoe water.

We take a brief break at a roadside rest at the crest of the summit before Wickenburg and eat a graham cracker or two. The refuse barrel is swarming with an amazing number of flies, and there's a pretty bad smell coming from it. I suggested to Randy that he look inside; he replied, "No, it might be something I'd have to report."

My favorite time to ride is late afternoons, with the golden light pouring over our shoulders. Especially this final afternoon, for several reasons: 1) when I saw the "Wickenburg 80" sign after the first hot ten miles, I never thought we'd make Wickenburg, and it's evident now we will, right on schedule for our 7 p.m. rendezvous; 2) it's a ten-mile descent; 3) it's beautiful, with mountains stacked against the horizon beyond the Hassayampa River basin; and, 4) we're all riding triumphantly together.

This so-called desert is rather verdant, with blooming mesquite trees growing in bushy rows along the highway since before Aguila. Some occasional staghorn cacti, and tall blooming century plants, but the desert floor between these showpieces is covered with low brown grass that looks like it was green not too long ago. Add the frequent irrigated fields, and stands of trees, and the dominant impression is of green growth, and plentiful water. Of course, granting the psychological nature of reality here, it probably will feel, and even look, different at high noon in July.

Just at dusk, the four of us roll past a historical marker commemorating an Apache massacre and into Wickenburg, "Dude Ranch Capital of the World." There, by the old hanging tree, is my high school buddy Alden, his Bronco set up with the four-place bicycle rack we sent him. Beers pop, panniers come off the bikes, and we're chauffeured 60 miles to the bright lights of Phoenix and a pizza dinner.

April 23rd and 24th   Days 7 and 8
Relaxing in Phoenix

I remember the first time I really thought of a cross-country tour. It was the night in May 1984 we spent at the Green Gables Inn in Pacific Grove during our tour down the California coast. The room was so very Victorian, and my little pocket radio was tuned to a public station playing some old swing band music, and I thought of the Mississippi River, and wanted to turn East and just keep pedalling.

Also heading toward the rising sun are Alden and his wife Diane, who will overtake us somewhere in their moving van on the way to Maine.

April 25th and 26th   Days 9 and 10
Still Relaxing

It feels like the Phoenix Metro area is being built up around us even as we drive through it, especially here in the rapidly-expanding Northeast. Rio Verde, where Nanci's parents have bought a home, is a lot of tile-roofed Spanish-style homes clustered around a couple of golf courses. The saguaros grow particularly thick hereabout, and there's one unusual thing: their delicate white blossoms, which I understood were only visible at night, persist into the late morning and early afternoon. Combined with the fire-tipped ocotillos, miscellaneous other flowers and the general golden bloom of the palo verde trees, the desert out here is particularly lush and other-worldly. I had expected the new Northway house to be somewhat starkly situated, but it's well shaded by large trees, ivy, and tall adobe walls, as if it's been here since the days of Don Diego.

Chapter Two:
Across the Center of the Universe

April 27th   Day 11
56.23 miles
Wickenburg — Prescott, Arizona

> If you would get exercise, go in search of the springs of life.
> Think of a man's swinging dumbbells for his health, when
> those springs are bubbling up in far-off pastures unsought
> by him!
>
> —Henry David Thoreau, "The Wild"

According to Don Dedera, former editor of *Arizona Highways*, there's a fellow somewhere around here named Charlie Pickrell who swears that when he was an undergraduate at the University of Arizona and heard his mother was dying in a Los Angeles hospital, he rode his bicycle to visit her. Charlie didn't have a car, nor much money either. Since his bike was his only valuable possession, he carried it up the hospital stairs to the intensive care ward, where a tire miraculously blew out, filling the room with healthy Arizona air. His mom recovered immediately, and Charlie rode her back home on the handlebars.

Nanci's Dad drove us in his rented car back to Wickenburg (2093'), from where we rode a rolling desert flat about 14 miles past saguaros and spiny Joshua trees to Congress (3025'), climbed Yarnall Hill (4783') overlooking the incredibly vast, hazy desert below, then rode across lush Peeples Valley, through the imperceptible towns of Wilhoit and Nowhere, and spiralled up a long hill into ponderosa pine country (6000') before a quick descent to Prescott.

Typical tricks of the terrain: the long stretch before the road divided on Yarnall Hill, and the long stretch approaching Wilhoit/Nowhere before the top-of-the-pines climb, both *appeared* level or slightly downhill, but we were cranking in low gears at 6-7 mph the whole way. Even the actual switchbacking climbs seemed easier—same gears, same speed—maybe because we were sheltered from the 10-15 mph SW sidewind. I still think it's more of a psychological than a physical barrier.

Both of us experienced some front-end wiggle on the descents. I ate one orange out of the front pack I suspected was overbalanced and presto, no more wiggle!

Skip and Diana had warned us to avoid the alternate route from Kirkland through Skull Valley to Prescott. They had been advised in Yarnall to take that route, but found it long and steep. We stopped in Yarnall for a cold drink to celebrate conquering its hill, and were relaxing in front of the grocery when up rode an older man in a helmet, his mountain bike equipped with high-rise handlebars, who told us that he'd never ridden either route but if he were going to, he'd take the alternate, because it's "smoother." We were polite but stuck to the main 89A, through Nowhere and up the unexpectedly long 12-mile grade to the pine country. Where the author of *Bicyclist's Guide to Arizona* had said "...a welcome 8-mile descent into Prescott..." it was more of a 4-mile descent, with the other four being some more steep uphill switchbacks.

But it's great to feel the chill in the air. After Yarnall, stopping in the shade is once more a cool proposition. In fact, climbing to Prescott, the terrain and climate were amazingly similar to climbing through the Coast Range, with prickly pears thrown in. Steep, brushy hillsides, with tall ponderosa pine and shorter pinon pine on the shadier slopes. And, like the Pacific Southwest, there's hardly any traffic.

It's fun to think that in one day we climbed from the saguaro and Joshua trees around Wickenburg to our cool pine-studded campsite a mile above Prescott—2000' to 6000', with some elevation lost and regained in there too. The White Spar Campground is pretty small and full of RVs, but it's the only one right on the road; several others a mile or so earlier are one and five miles off the road (to the right). Maybe paved, maybe not; probably steep one way or the other. There's a section at White Spar marked ROAD CLOSED but we sneak our bikes past the sign and a locked gate and cook our whole wheat macaroni and cheese in splendid solitude on the concrete picnic table.

Another wonderful thing is the water. Since Yarnall it has been pure delicious spring-type; no more salty desert brew.

April 28th   Day 12
46.2 miles
Prescott — Cottonwood, Arizona

More motorized two-wheeled recreation has whizzed by us on the way up to Prescott (remember to pronounce it "Press-kitt"). The next morning there's a huge gathering of motocross riders on the outskirts of town in their colorful padded garb. We roll through this mile-high Western burg ("with a veneer of contemporary resort," says the guidebook) and stop at the Waffle Iron, where I ate two buckwheat Belgian waffles with fresh fruit and yoghurt. The Sunday morning brunch crowd is moving in as we leave.

Some steep rolling sections out of town, with a lovely passage through red granite boulders where 89A takes off to the right. We ride down to somewhere near 4000' across a big open valley, with a brief vision of the snowy San Francisco Peaks before the newly-developed ranch homes of Prescott Valley and then the steep start of the climb over broad

Mingus Mountain. A huge plume of white smoke off the ridge makes me wonder what we'd do if the road were closed by a fire. But the road snakes up into a lush valley, giving us discouraging glimpses of the roadcuts far above our heads. It is Sunday, and there's definitely some weekend traffic. We stop several times for water and rest. The scent of pines is refreshing.

From the top of the grade to the north we have an awesome view of the Mogollon Rim, striated in reddish sandstones and stretching like an enormous curbstone across the horizon. Twin white pyramids of the San Francisco Peaks protrude beyond. Below is the thickly-vegetated line of the Verde River running through Cottonwood, which from here looks like a big town. The lighter, tan stone above the red stratum is dotted with those short pines, giving the whole a real Arizona look reminiscent of the Grand Canyon. We swoop down some exciting curves, hitting nearly 40 mph, through a beautiful little green valley, then ... surprise! up again for a half-mile, then it's down for sure, through some of that red rock, then rounding a sharp left turn for a sudden, totally unexpected entrance into the arty little former mining town of Jerome.

The town is literally hanging on the hillside, with houses on the uphill side looming over reinforced banks, and on the downhill side set so one looks out over their roofs, to the Verde Valley below. Sharp downhill curves lead into the main part of town, where on a side street we discover Maude's Cafe, a little basement place from where we can look up through the door to see our bikes chained to a lamppost. Maude's been in business six years, serving homemade everything (including the mayonnaise). Each of us has a green salad with poppyseed dressing, then I have a bowl of minestrone with little bits of ham, and some cheese blintzes grilled in butter and smothered in sour cream with apricot preserves alongside. Also homemade lemonade, a cappuccino, a piece of walnut torte with shortbread crust, and a brownie. Nanci had a sandwich or something; I didn't notice. Maude herself was eccentric and loudspoken, quoting lines from *Julius Caesar* to explain something to one of her employees. "The fault, dear Jennifer, lies not in our customers..."

After that I went around town taking pictures, then Nanci shopped—

we took turns roaming and watching the bikes. In the park, a tiny affair overhanging the main street, I spoke with a group of beer-drinking recreational motorcyclists, in particular one German-accented fellow named Berk. A drunkenly exuberant group of young and middle-aged men from Flagstaff, they were riding the latest machines, Japanese bikes with enclosed engines. Leaning over the railing that overlooked the sidewalk, this "Sunday (or Sunny) Afternoon Club," as they called themselves, made loud comments to passing women, who ignored them, until finally someone dropped a full can of beer the half-story to the pavement. I sidled away, so as not to be blamed by the throngs of tourists wandering around the antique stores and art galleries.

There are too many cars in the narrow cobblestone streets to preserve that really "historic" look. One large, shirtless young man with a New York face and accent asked me, "Say, you know where that concert is, where Kathleen's singing?" I had an eerie feeling of living there in a past life. How long does it take to become a certified Jerome local? An hour?

Odd facts about Jerome: founded in 1867, named by Winston Churchill Jr.'s mother's cousin; the young Pancho Villa's first job was bringing water to town on muleback from nearby springs.

Soon we bounced out of town on the cobblestones, the road smoothing and leading us down in a series of tight curves to Clarkdale, past Tuzigoot National Monument, and then to Cottonwood. Big sign at city limits: PEDDLERS MUST REGISTER. Pedalers too? The motorcyclists slowed down to yell encouragement as they passed. We followed my friend Roger's mother Ruth's directions to his house on Main Street, where he'd draped his mailbox in red, white and blue bunting and posted a welcome sign loaded with typical Firesign Theater allusions. We were glad to see Mr. Copley and partake of his beer, shower, music and good cheer. Dinner at Vince's, out in Cornville, where the eccentric waitress Peggy served us linguine with clam sauce, garlic bread, red wine, and homemade spumoni. She plumped down beside me to take our order, spoke in a dazed drawl, and called water "white lightning." Food okay but not superb, and expensive. Back at Roger's we passed out listening to his vintage recording of *The Adventures of Nick Danger*.

Next morning Roger, who works for the Postal Service, had to drop his mail jeep off at his assistant Mo's, who lived next to the Dugout Restaurant where we ate a thoroughly ordinary breakfast. Roger decided to ride with us, and with him lagging behind (his body has been debilitated by years of abuse) we crossed the Verde River and climbed the 16 miles to Sedona. To our dismay, the road was heavily used by commercial traffic, winding often shoulderless into the spectacular red rock country. The scenery was increasingly beautiful but we were terrified by the continuous stream of campers and tractor-trailers. Somehow we made it, stopping at Beverly's Market for carrot juice, bagels, spicy cheese and other food-to-go from this friendly little fruit stand.

I remember Sedona from 1971-72 as a small, out-of-the-way country town with lots of low-rent ramshackle housing for students from nearby Prescott College. Now, it's a sprawling four-lane series of fashionable developments, restaurants, fast food, and real estate offices.

Just beyond it, though, is the entrance to Oak Creek Canyon, a 12-mile winding road, encased in greenery, that climbs through this giant cut in the Mogollon Rim. Still plenty of traffic, including some buses, but everybody's going pretty slow so we feel better. We stopped early on and climbed down to the creek for lunch; hot on the road, but cool in the shade. Gradually as we got deeper into the canyon the scrubby vegetation and cottonwoods gave way to tall pines. Although it wasn't totally evident, we were climbing a thousand feet above the level of Sedona. At the end of the canyon, the climb got serious—three miles of steep switchbacks climbing another 1500' to the top.

Different styles of climbing: I tend to drop right on to my lowest sprockets and gladly spin the whole way in my 27" gear, while Nanci likes to keep a gear or two in reserve, and cranks more when climbing.

At the top it's full-on pines, lining the straight but hilly road 12 miles into Flagstaff. I went ahead to gather info on campsites and the upcoming Indian reservations, while Nanci waited at the top of the switchbacks for Roger. We reunited at Kathy's Cafe in downtown "Flag," and since it was too dark for a basically unknown ride to Sunset Crater National Monument, we used the first four of our Holiday Inn scrip, a present from my parents, for a double room, $37.50 + $10 extra person.

We were the only customers at Kathy's, where we had fruit smoothies, salads, and dinner of acorn squash stuffed with apples, raisins and walnuts, and chicken breast sauteed in ginger teriyaki with mandarin oranges. I went out to find a bottle of wine, but the nearby package store offered only products of the wrong countries—Mateus and Reunite. But then Kathy herself donated a bottle of North Coast Blanc de Blancs. Nice, dimly-lit, earthy, wooden cafe. Kathy a little bit scattered, blond, smokes BelAirs, into Scientology (quotes L. Ron Hubbard on the menu).

April 29th   Day 13
71.03 miles
Flagstaff — Cameron, Arizona

We return to Kathy's for breakfast the next morning at 6:30: buckwheat pancakes, fresh fruit, o.j., potatoes, etc. Place is crowded, and one customer is Berk from the motorcycle club I met in Jerome, now dressed like a stockbroker.

In spite of our early start, we fiddle around getting film, taking photos, mailing cards and film, until 9 a.m. Roger says goodbye and heads back toward Cottonwood, and we turn into a horrible busy street, Route 66, then 89 North through East Flagstaff. The highway is under construction, and choking clouds of dirt blow across the road with the wind that several times knocks me into the soft dirt on the shoulder. Lots of big trucks. It's flat, or even slightly downhill, but the crosswind cancels any advantage. Snowcapped San Francisco Peaks recede to our left, as we struggle to stay on the road. A short climb, then the turnoff to Sunset and Wupatki National Monuments. No more traffic, and it's a beautiful, solitary ride through forests and meadows. We pause to recoup at the Sunset Crater Visitors' Center.

From there we climbed slightly past lava flows and craters, and Sunset Crater itself, to a view northward across the craters to the land below, flattened and displaying the reds, pinks, and browns of the Painted Desert. A long, low cliff-edged mesa ran across the horizon. We descended in long curves, then ran out along near-flat, piñon-juniper country. It's amazing to see ponderosa, piñon, and other big trees growing out of the black volcanic soil, but then we learned that the cinders act as both mulch and fertilizer.

At Wupatki numerous exhibits displayed the cross-cultural nature of the land: people from all directions came in around 650 A.D. to take advantage of the fertility and water—Hohokam, Anastazi, and Sinagua (Spanish, "without water"), among others. The ruins of their pueblos, including ballcourts, are scattered over the area. They were flourishing until 1250 AD and later, the eruption of Sunset in 1150 only adding to the area's popularity, though the people did have to move down off the higher ground near the active volcanoes. Molds of corncobs were found in some of the lava flows.

We fought a terrible headwind out of Wupatki back to 89 North—18 miles at 4-7 mph, with some short steep grades to make it worse. Standing out of the saddle in bottom gear, grunting, the wind must have been a steady 20-25 mph, with gusts. Some high clouds on the Western horizon. The land is flat and rolling now, grassy, with diminishing shrubbery. Nanci says, "The sky suddenly got big." Purple loco weed lines the roadway.

Once on 89 the headwind turns into a tailwind and we do the 22 miles to Cameron at 25-30 mph. Not much shoulder for awhile but when we cross into the reservation suddenly there's an excellent one. Some ragtag motels and a cafe at Grey Mountain, and if we hadn't talked to some bicycle tourists headed up from the Grand Canyon to Tucson, we never would have guessed that Cameron offered anything more than similar roadside sleaze.

It feels like a different country already. We're in the Cameron Trading Post "Motel" (more of a hotel, actually), a striking two-story building of local red rock with the roof timbers protruding, Pueblo-style. Inside, the lobby is all polished wood and stone, and our room—$20.70!—is in the Zuni Court, a separate building whose rooms all open into an interior courtyard where there's a big stone grill. Everything is overgrown with vines and huge cottonwoods shelter the main building. The dining room, past a huge display of Indian jewelry, rugs, sand paintings, pottery, and tourist gewgaws, is also furnished with top quality woodwork, long shelving across the walls displaying Navajo art, and above there's an immense stamped-tin ceiling. The dining room is only a year old, but the hotel, I'm told, was built in 1910. All the employees of this tribal-owned enterprise are Indians.

I had a huge Navajo taco for $3.75. Our spacious room reminds me a little of the Ahwanee Hotel in Yosemite Valley, with Indian-design bedspreads and one wooden wall, TV (but no phone), and the bathroom decked out in hardware-store wooden and brass fixtures: oak toilet seat, etc. All in flawless repair, or else very new. The ornate overhead toilet tank flushes loudly.

We do feel somewhat apprehensive about crossing the reservations. Campgrounds are scarce, and various sources—maps, US Forest Service, guidebooks—disagree on where they are. We are warned that tribal regulations forbid BLM-style free camping, and a fellow at the North Face store in Phoenix warned us not to camp anywhere near the road if we do. Stories abound of drunken Indians in pickup trucks, and the ranger at Wupatki National Monument Visitor Center even told us, bless her soul, of a female bicyclist with an organized group who was pulled off the road near Tuba City and raped. "But it's nothing to worry about," she kindly added.

April 30th   Day 14
83 miles
Cameron — Second Mesa, Arizona

So far, so good here in Indian country. We left at 7 a.m. after the usual pancakes, and rolled down through the dawn, then up a couple of steep grades, to Tuba City—25 miles in two hours. Crossed the Little Colorado gorge right out of Cameron, then climbed gently past numerous booths selling jewelry and rugs— JEWRIES FOR SALE   reads one hand-painted signboard. Turning off 89 we lost most of the traffic but the smooth shoulder went away too and the road is now rent with cracks, often with grass growing in them. Where they've been patched is a bump, and if not patched, then a thump. Big new Teec Nos Pos Shopping Plaza in Tuba City, but not much bike equipment in the Yellow Front. I called the Hopi Cultural Center at Second Mesa to make reservations, casting the die by giving my VISA number. We turned on the Hopi road for what proved to be a lot of mesa-climbing: a small one, then Coal Mine, then Howell, then Third, then Second. Various views but nothing really colorful except the red rock on either side of Tuba. Here and there are settlements visible from the road—mostly trailers and cinderblock houses.

Sun's strong but not too hot. Very light traffic, but same terrible road. Our anxiety has shifted from imaginary threats and drunk drivers to the distance we must cover, which according to the map and our other info is 94 miles, or 69 from Tuba. Turns out to be about 10 miles less, which thanks to some descents and flat stretches with tailwinds we complete by 5 p.m. Passed Old Oraibi, oldest continuously-occupied settlement in North America (since 1100 A.D.). From our route it looked like a cluster of flat brown adobe condominiums. Later I heard that, for the first time since the early 20th century, no tourists will be allowed to view the annual Snake Dance the Hopis still perform to bring the winter rains. Although we didn't see them, there are supposed to be signs on the turnoffs to the pueblos that say   NO WHITES.

More traffic, then one final long climb, which we are psychologically unprepared for, to the Cultural Center in Second Mesa. This is apparently still west of the actual town of Second Mesa, as pinpointed on the map. Lots of tourists around.

The Cultural Center is built pueblo-style, with cement walls and several courtyards with old wooden doors on the rooms. It looked kind of like a prison or school when we rode up. A room for two is $33, TV extra. We relax in the room, the radio tuned to a college station from Flagstaff playing Copland's   Sonata for Violin & Piano.

The dining room menu has some Hopi specialties, including *nok qui vi,* a lamb stew with big hominy kernels, rich broth, fry bread on the side, and a single roasted green chile. Had an order of piki bread, a paper-thin, phyllo-like bread made from blue corn, and colored a deep gray-green. Rest of food is truck stop-style, except for a salad bar. Most of the Hopis seem mildly friendly; they dress differently than the silver and turquoise-laden Navajo, with more colored cloth, a cloth-belted black shawl around one shoulder over a blouse. Maybe it's because the

Hopis have always been a sedentary tribe, while the Navajo have had to make the transition from mobile raiders to homeowners. All over the news now is the big land squabble between the two tribes, roots of which go back to Spanish occupation of the area. Hopi reservation is surrounded by huge Navajo reservation the size of West Virginia—there's even some small Navajo sections within the encircled Hopi land. We saw some trucks carrying furniture and mattresses—relocating?

May 1st   Day 15
89 miles
Second Mesa — Summit Campground, Arizona

Next morning we ate breakfast—*nova* in Hopi—at the Cultural Center: blue cornmeal pancakes. Saw blue cornflakes at nearby tables. Afterwards we shopped for silver and walked through the museum, seeing old black and white photos of Hopi life. For awhile the museum sound system had some corny country pop playing, then it was replaced by some traditional Indian chants, pentatonic, kind of like a slowed-up "Fanfare for the Common Man," and I could hear the woman behind the counter singing along. Hopis have a kind of overlay technique in their silverwork that was apparently developed relatively recently, after World War II, in a deliberate effort to encourage traditional crafts among them.

Despite the Navajo Nation's size and immense bureaucratic organization, the Hopi (they say *Hopid*) seem to have a greater cultural identity. The Navajos are cowboys, or shepherds, or just roughnecks, while the Hopis are farmers. Their rituals are locked into the land and its seasons, beginning with the winter solstice and running into July with its pre-harvest festivities. A series of visits by the Kachinas, spirit guides from the sacred San Francisco Peaks (whose snowcapped summits remained visible from all the mesa tops) initiates a cycle of dances: comic performances by the Mudheads; the Snake Dance, in which the Snake Priests hold live rattlesnakes in their mouths while moving around a sacred circle of blue cornmeal, to ensure the rains; and the Niman or home dance, thanking the Kachinas for their gifts, following which the

Kachinas all fly home.

Among Hopis, the men do all the weaving while the women do pottery and make baskets. The potters taste the clay, using only sweet clay and never salty or bitter clay. They are dry farmers, using no irrigation. Their faces are sharper than the broad Navajo visage, and to me, they seem friendlier.

Cruising off Second Mesa, some high cloudiness gave us relief from the sun. Stopped to shop at a rather large, well-stocked market in the town of Second Mesa, then continued around the foot of narrow First Mesa, past a huge new school, past a sign marking the boundary between the Hopi lands and the resumption of the Navajo reservation, and into the town of Keams Canyon. Very bad road surface here.

Keams is narrow, nestled between colorful sandstone cliffs, and very busy. Big store, and people selling jewelry and rugs in the park. Climbed a steep hill out of the canyon, short level section, then another steep climb, and abruptly the country changed. From the rocky, bushy barrenness of the mesas we were suddenly in sagebrush, with plenty of juniper and piñon about. Everything seemed greener. The mountains on the eastern horizon were clearly forested. Some long rolling descents and climbs, and finally we reached our goal, Ganado, only to discover that there were no campgrounds (we were told) and no motels (they laughed when we asked). It was 5:30 p.m., and no choice but a long climb from 6400' to Summit Campground, 19 miles away and 1350 feet higher.

We watered up and rode it, a beautiful sunset in our rear-view mirrors, but it got darker and darker until we had to put on our reflective jackets for safety as well as warmth. The piñons grew taller and thicker, until Ponderosa pines showed up at 7000'. It was so dark we weren't sure where the campground was; it turned out to be a glorified roadside rest area at the junction of the road to Sawmill and Antelope Lake. We made kind of a nervous camp, no tent, some ways back from the busy road full of high-speed pickups, trying to make sure we weren't sacking out on a side road. Good sleep, though, even with no dinner, and an amazing sky full of stars and cosmic dust.

Right before Ganado, at Burnside Junction, where we would have turned north for Canyon de Chelly had we not decided to skip that sightseeing detour, we stopped for rubbery french fries and Snickers bars at the corner gas mart, and were accosted by Glenn Tsosie, an obviously inebriated Navajo talking through an immense mouthful of tobacco, who said he had been a staff sergeant in the Vietnam War.

"You watch out," he warned. "Most Indians are good, but there's some bad ones." (A mile back, during our high-speed descent, a couple of young Navajos slowed down to have a conversation first with me, then Nanci. "Time to put my sweatshirt on," she said.) Learning we were from the California mountains, Glenn said he thought it was good that mountain people lived like Indians, without utilities, in small out-of-the-way cabins. I didn't tell him how we ranted and raved every time the power went out or the pipes froze. He gave us his address and asked us to write. We shook hands, and did write him a postcard later on.

May 2nd   Day 16
38 miles
Summit Campground, Arizona — Gallup, New Mexico

Next day was an early, cold one, with thick dark clouds creating a pearly sunrise. We were glad to discover in the light that we actually had been in a campground of sorts. The sign at the summit said "Elevation 7750." We rolled 12 miles downhill to Window Rock, a big, busy place and the capital of the Navajo Nation, for breakfast. The forested plateau from which we had just descended is the southern tip of the Chuska Mountains, we learned from a Navajo woman having her morning coffee. She'd pray for us, she said. Christian missionaries are very active through all these reservations, even though quite a few tribes including the Hopis and Navajos rose up in 1680 and killed all the Catholic priests who were busy trying to replace their rituals with Rome's.

We know we're near New Mexico because Nanci's chili omelette is smothered in green chile, hot and very good. Plenty of traffic from here, 26 miles to Gallup. The road, which got very smooth out of Ganado and over the summit, loses its shoulder, and now we're dodging trucks again. A few spits of rain. We hit Gallup, "Heart of Indian Country," and hightail it to the Holiday Inn, arriving at noon. Clouds still threaten, and it's gusty riding west along Old 66. Now we're lounging at our motel, doing laundry, writing cards, working on bikes, and generally spending the long afternoon resting our legs as I think it will be necessary to do once a week or so.

We made friends with Richard, a young boy on a BMX. The prototype of the chatty, never-leave-you-alone kid, he's loitering by the entrance to the Holiday Inn, and talks bike talk about his bike and his Dad's mountain bike, even while I'm out by the dumpsters mechanicking. Our bikes seem in pretty good shape; a few loose bolts and dirty chains are the most serious details.

May 3rd Day 17
62 miles
Gallup — El Morro, New Mexico

For breakfast we decided to ride in search of Earl's, which we had read about in *Good Food* by Michael and Jane Stern. Six miles east on Old 66, there is the sign—"We Serve the Nicest People" for what is billed as the epitome of truck stop food. But it's too ordinary, the only good points being nice "floofy" pancakes, far from the flat and rubbery ones we'd been getting, and the thermos pot of coffee on the table. Hashbrowns were pretty bad, although at least there was no rancid grease. The waitress, who is harried and whom I overheard saying she's losing her mind, forgets to charge us for one order—an informal two-for-one. Somehow I don't feel like correcting the bill. A disappointment.

Climbing out of Gallup, a town all on the wrong side of the tracks, we see plenty of destitute characters lounging about early this Saturday morning. We're soon heading southeast and climbing slowly into piñon and ponderosa, finally entering the Zuni reservation. It's somehow different than the Hopi or Navajo areas—more stores and cafes. Long descent to the intersection with the road west to Zuni; we turn east, finally with the wind at our backs, and climb gradually again, past numerous houses built from blocks of red rock. Dark clouds gathering overhead, so at about 2 p.m., as a few drops of rain start to fall, we pull over beneath some piñons and put covers on our panniers, trash bags over the tent and sleeping bags, and rainjackets and pants on us. But despite some heavy fireworks (one bolt hits real close, seeming to send a sizzling spark along the barbed wire fence) no real rain develops, and the raingear proves to be a very effective personal sauna. So we soon strip back down to T-shirts and shorts as we pedal into the Ramah Valley.

Short passage through some roadwork, and it's like a bad dream to force our skinny tires through the gluey, tarry surface.

Ramah is in a lush, green valley between mesas. Some old stone houses beneath giant arching cottonwoods. I stop at the grocery on the far side of town to get some Zuni sour bread for $1.95 a 1-1/4 pound loaf. More activity here than would seem to match the size of the town: a large school, posters of meetings, music, etc.; the attractive counter woman saying to a customer, "Okay, well, we'll have to wait till Francisco is finished to call a committee meeting, and I don't know when ..."

Soon we cross a low pass and descend across a huge valley with the 200-foot white cliff of El Morro ahead against the dark sky. To the left some red sandstone towers at the edge of a faroff mesa are dramatically lit. Closer and closer, till we turn right into El Morro National Monument. Camp, unbelievably at no charge, in a beautiful site on a pine-forested knoll with views of El Morro and neighboring cliffs. It's almost 5 p.m., so no time to hike and only a short trip to the Visitor Center. It's a few hundred yards on a short unpaved road to camp, where we pitch the tent in a strong breeze, and cook pasta shells (from Sedona) with cheese sauce and Zuni bread, which turns out to be much like a crusty, chewy San Francisco sourdough.

A few drops of rain, making our tent about the coziest place to be.

May 4th   Day 18
45.5 miles
El Morro — Grants, New Mexico

Next morning we arose from our excellent camp in the junipers, ate hot rice cereal with dates, packed up, and headed for the Visitor Center. El Morro ("The Bluff" in Spanish) is the world's largest wall of graffiti, with prehistoric petroglyphs above messages carved by Spanish and American passers-by from 1609 on. (The older inscriptions are higher because the ground at the base of the cliff has gradually eroded away.) Don Diego de Varga's markings are some of the most prominent: "...having reconquered Zuni at my own expense for the Queen of Spain..." Some other Spaniards left expense reports too, often humorously defaced by their contemporaries. This cliff, with its attendant pool of run-off supplying the only dependable water for many miles, was a popular stopping place for various army detachments and emigrant trains: Spanish patrols sent to subdue or resubdue Zuni and Hopi pueblos, or avenge the killings of priests; American Lt. Edward F. Beale, who in 1857 was sent to test camels for desert use (from here to Quartzsite?); and groups of California-bound emigrants. One 65-year-old man, leaving the East to visit his sons in Sacramento, left his marks and made it as far as the Colorado River, where their wagon train was attacked and burned by the natives. They fled on foot back to Albuquerque (hundreds of miles), recouped, then repeated the trip, this time without incident. The man was reunited with his children and died in Sacramento at a very advanced age.

We walked a two-mile trail around the base of the cliff, past the deep green pool set into the sandstone wall, and past the rows of inscriptions, guided by a pamphlet telling us these and many more stories of the carvings. Then the trail climbed the rock for a sweeping view of the surrounding country, which like most of the West was underwater millions of years ago. The large, low Zuni mountains, almost plateaus, stretched to the north and east. A few cinder cones poked up to the south. Perched on top of El Morro were Zuni ruins, mostly unexcavated. What a great defensive location!

After the walk we rode ten miles further up an easy grade to the Continental Divide (7885'). Will this be our final high point of the trip? Close to it, anyway. Then a long fast descent, mostly north by northeast, through twisted black lava beds, past a sign pointing to "Ice Caves," and into Grants. Quite a fierce wind was coming out of the south-southwest by then, and when the road temporarily turned west, we had to fight for every revolution of the pedals.

Right before Interstate 40 at Grants was the Cibola Sands RV Park, offering some rather exposed tent spaces. We continued over the freeway and turned east to ride through Grants, a sad little town but a long one. Another gypsum plant (sign on door: NOT HIRING), and only one shopping center well off the main road to the north. We rode to the far side of town and a row of big motels. Holiday Inn had just changed ownership ("Holiday Grants"?—good luck!) and wouldn't take our scrip, so we went next door to the Motel 6: $25 for two. But the room was stripped to essentials, with no drawers, a shower stall but no tub, and a non-functioning Magic Fingers in which I lost a quarter (intended as a decorative Pop Art antique?).

We went next door to a big fancy Best Western for drinks to celebrate crossing the Great Divide, and I got sloshed on two enormous 75-cent beers. We overheard two truck drivers talking to the bartender, a nice pudgy woman, and each other. Each had a load of autos, and one old pipe-sucking fellow was taking his load of Cadillacs to Scottsdale, Arizona, a wealthy suburb of Phoenix. Both were tired of fighting the wind. They talked about how they took back roads, shifted gears, and cheated in their logbooks. The old fellow said he'd be late now with his delivery, to which the other commented: "Thass all right. They's enough Cadillacs in Scottsdale already."

We ate dinner there too, seafood and prime rib. Not very busy; just a few travelers. Pretty good country-western band, with electric fiddle, started up in the lounge about 7 p.m. We retired to the Motel 6 before long.

May 5th   Day 19 — Cinco de Mayo!
98.4 miles
Grants — Coronado State Park, New Mexico

Next morning, our earliest start yet, we hit the House of Pancakes while it was still dark at 5:30 a.m. for a big, sweet breakfast from a giggly waitress. It was cold there at 6500' above the sea, but luckily the wind was dormant. Back on the road, we turned east on unmarked Old Highway 66, which soon cut south across the freeway by a Stuckey's.

It looked like it continued south from there, curving up into the hills, so we chose the freeway shoulder; after a few hundred yards, however, the road reappeared below us to the right. We skidded down the bank and continued along the deserted two-lane road at a good clip, into the Acuna Indian reservation, crossing the freeway and moving right past the old Acuna pueblo, the town of San Fidel, and so forth. Mostly dilapidated old motels and service stations, some bars by the road, and humble houses back in the rocks and brush.

After New Laguna was Old Laguna at the bottom of a hill, where we stopped at the market for our juice break and to stock up on some cheese for lunch. While we were standing in the sun, an old Indian man, John, who worked at the adjacent service station, came up to us and told us how to stay on the frontage road at the next interchange. This part of the road took us far to the north of the freeway, through some beautiful red rock bluffs and cliffs, finally rejoining the interstate where we had to give up and get on it. We had a 28-mile ride on I-40, a terribly rough, gravelly shoulder that just got worse. We entered a construction zone: CAUTION SHOULDER WORK AHEAD —my first thought was, good, it needs work. Then I thought, oh no, it's all we've got to ride on! They had perforated the pavement with some machine—preparatory, I guess, to laying down a new surface. Rough going, threading a few barriers and dodging a few trucks.

But we made good time with our tailwind, and it wasn't too soon before we got to the Rio Puerco exit where our frontage road continued. Lunched on some substantial Navajo tacos at a little restaurant in Rio Puerco. The frontage road continued all the way to the last hill overlooking Albuquerque, where it crossed over to the south side, became Central Avenue, and gave us a 45 mph descent into town.

At the top of the hill before Albuquerque, while we were getting oriented for our descent into the city, a black man in a beret pulled up in an old sedan next to a neighboring mobile home lot. He pulled out some drums and played for awhile.

This from Willa Cather's *Death Comes for the Archbishop:* during Spanish rule in the early 18th century, the priest at the Acoma Pueblo, on the cliff above present-day I-40, invited four other padres from nearby pueblos to ride out for dinner, so as to have someone to admire his elaborate setup. When the padres arrived, they found beautiful gardens, watered from jugs the Indian women carried up on their heads from the river far below. A turkey was cooking on a spit. When it was time to eat, the priest clapped his hands and a small Indian boy hurried over with the turkey. Suddenly, the boy tripped and fell, spilling the meat on the floor. In a rage the host struck the boy, killing him. The other priests left immediately. That night all was silence at the Acoma Pueblo. At about three in the morning, they came for the priest and threw him off the cliff.

We went straight to Old Town and parked in the plaza. Each of us shopped while the other guarded the bikes. I sat there and met Roberto Sandoval, whose son has a bike. Roberto was very interested in our gear, but didn't think he'd like touring. "You just drink water, eh? None of this?" tilting an imaginary bottle to his lips. Roberto, wearing baseball shirt and cap, is missing some teeth and is kind of hard to understand. Short, slim, he's one of several Hispanics with no clear purpose, hanging around this tree-shaded plaza on Cinco de Mayo. (Today's Monday, so most of the festivities took place yesterday.) Sunny, nice breeze (in our direction). Some touristy shops and restaurants around. And, of course, tourists—of different nationalities, hairstyles, dress—many in shorts and skimpy blouses exposing chests more daringly than we're used to in the Southwestern hinterlands.

As Nanci returns, we also start talking with Darryl from Pennsylvania. A real friendly guy, who has lived in Lancaster County with the Amish.

Riding out of Albuquerque along the Rio Grande isn't much fun. Although we quickly leave the busy central district, entering into a wealthy district of horse ranches and expensive-looking developments, the road has no shoulder and there's a lot of traffic. We cut east to 85, which gets better the further north we go, and then we start passing pueblos, the biggest being Sandia with its old church. Beautiful big cottonwoods grow along the road and the Sandia Crest to the east is lit in the lowering sun. Soon (17 miles) we're in Bernalillo, where we stop at the Unfinished Cafe and Bakery. It's run by hip young whites (who seem to occupy this town in equal proportion to the Hispanics), and we buy a poppy seed pretzel and a bag of day-old croissants for $1.50. Thus provisioned (Nanci also buys some vegetables down the street at the T & T while I write postcards), we ride a couple of miles northwest to Coronado State Monument, the nicest state campground we've ever been to. Right on the Rio Grande, with little adobe shelters for each site (five no hookup, seven with hookup), it's great, and the Sandia Crest's looming over the leisurely river. We meet Linda, the polo groom, who's camping next to us, cooking a small amount of something that looks like onions and sliced apples in a battered aluminum pot over a camp stove.

Linda's a good-looking gal with a rough and ready manner, driving a mini-pickup with Texas plates. She gives me a couple Michelobs, one of which I dunk in the river to cool using strips of a yellow plastic bag to tie it to a branch (the river is down a steep bank from the campsite) and the other I pop open right away and drink while Linda, Frank Guitterez the ranger, myself and soon Nanci toast Cinco de Mayo and talk about a variety of things. The wind dies and it's a nice evening. Frank takes Linda out for dinner. Nanci and I eat pasta, shower, and pass out.

May 6th   Day 20
44.6 miles
Coronado — Sante Fe, New Mexico

Next morning we strike camp and go to check out the ruins. This was where Coronado and a huge army, exploring north from Old Mexico in search of the Seven Cities of Gold, spent the winter.

The Indians got so overburdened with the conquistadors' demands that in the mid-16th century they rebelled, albeit without success. Coronado, of course, went on to discover seven cities of mud, killed his untrustworthy Indian guide, and returned in failure. He was later tried for mismanagement of the army and, incredibly for that time, cruelty to the native peoples, but although he was acquitted he never realized the fame he would attain centuries later.

In one of the unearthed kivas archaeologists found a set of murals, which were salvaged, restored, and now are on display in a wing of the visitor center. You can climb down into a restored kiva here, among the low masonry ruins (not unlike South Bronx urban devastation) and see replicas of the murals in their authentic setting. Usual wooden ladder poking out of the sunken rooftop, one pole always longer than the other.

This pueblo was at one time 5-6 stories high, housing hundreds, perhaps at one time thousands, of native Americans. Early Spanish explorers report that the men put the wooden beams into place, while the women applied the mud. They'd pile up grass and brush, burn it to ashes, then mix it with mud and slap it on. They also made blocks of it. The men, by the way, did the weaving and spinning in this culture too. Their pueblo was in the Tiguey province, and as the population dwindled (disease) the people moved away to other pueblos, some of them downriver to Sandia, according to the current residents of that pueblo.

Nice museum next to the murals in the visitor center, with a suit of Spanish armor available for try-on. Helmet's too small for me and it's hard to imagine wearing that heavy breastplate through a New Mexican summer. Image, too, of the tonsured priest padding along in sandals behind the military train, cross in hand, perhaps some Indian converts with him. Or the priest on donkeyback. Whichever, there was apparently increasing conflict between the Spanish state and the Catholic Church during this time of conquest and colonization. Priests became champions of the natives against depredations of greedy *alcaldes*, military commanders, and soldiers. The army protected the holy fathers, and the latter helped pacify the conquered Indians, but did not endear themselves to the practical men of action.

Conflict persists today, as we learned from Frank the ranger. Part of the campground closest to the monument is closed because a neighboring pueblo wants to annex the riverside land, and a civil suit is pending.

The day is another bright and sunny one with some wind. Linda went on her way to Sante Fe and Taos to meet with her riverrunner boyfriend and float the Rio Grande gorge below Taos, and we finished our breakfast pasta and started up I-25 frontage roads, past more pueblos, towards Sante Fe. Soon we had to get on the interstate, which wasn't bad except for lots of broken glass and other highway debris (cigarette butts, straps, metal pieces, baby diapers, tire fragments). Also, we were gaining 2000 feet as we climbed out of the river, and we felt it—only 45 miles but felt like 145, especially compared to the previous day's 98, which seemed easy.

Had to abandon the frontage road at Algodones, although it looked like we could have taken it as far as San Felipe (it went far to the west there by that pueblo). At La Cienega ("the descent" in Spanish), finally, we saw Sante Fe against the still-snowy Sangre de Cristo range (the range had been intermittently visible in the far distance since before Albuquerque). Stopped at a tourist information center for brochures, maps, other info including location of AAA. Not a descent like into Albuquerque, but much more rolling. The frontage road we were back on by then veered to the right and joined Route 14 on which we first biked into this area in May 1983 with Skip and Diana. The road comes from the restored mining town of Madrid, connecting Sante Fe with Albuquerque along a more mountainous and scenic route, which we traversed back then in a day and a half. We turned left on it now, went under the freeway, and ended up on Cerillos Road, an impossibly busy main artery with little shoulder. We had to ride quite a ways into town on it, stopping by the AAA office for a resupply of traveler's checks.

There at the AAA office we spoke with an older guy who had the desire to ride from Albuquerque to San Diego (not recommended by us due to prevailing winds!) and we learned of Grant Corner Inn, a bed & breakfast one block from the plaza. The rest of the ride on Cerillos was better, especially when we entered the downtown area and motels and fast food were replaced by adobe churches and government buildings.

The inn is a restored Victorian home built in 1905. Our hosts, Pat and Louise Stewart, had gained quite a bit of notoriety with their gourmet breakfasts as well as lodging ($65 and up for two). Their employee Komala, a pleasant, portly woman, showed us room #2, by the back door across from the kitchen. It was Tuesday afternoon, but they were fairly busy. We unloaded our gear, locked the bikes in a basement stairwell, showered, changed, and relaxed with glasses of wine while leafing through menus of local restaurants. We settled on La Casa Sena for this first night.

Located within the Plaza Sena adjoining the main plaza, the restaurant was decorated in Southwestern pastels. Hip people surrounded us, but our waitress was really nice—not "superhip." She tipped us off to local bike shops and outdoor specialists, and we tipped her in return.

Cajun-style cooking has made it this far: Nanci had red snapper blackened with New Mexican spices, and I had Pollo Eugenie—chicken breasts in Maytag blue cheese sauce over blue cornbread. We also had some fresh oysters, and I had jalapeño black bean soup. In addition, a bottle of Alexander Valley 1984 Chardonnay. Dessert was a piece of avocado-lime pie, shared between us.

Afterwards we wandered into the restaurant's cantina, where an excellent pianist was improvising on "Willow Weep for Me." After a few turns around the plaza, peering through the shop windows at pottery and Indian blankets, we let ourselves into Grant Corner with our key and retired.

May 7th   Day 21
A Leisurely Day Off

Next morning I was up at 6:30 for early coffee and a round of furious writing (trying to catch up on this damn thing *and* write a piece for the newspapers back home). Nanci was soon up and doing a load of laundry at a nearby laundromat while I continued writing.

More on Sante Fe: the core of the town, including many government and state buildings, is striking because it's all made of adobe. The pinkish brown walls, protruding beams, and distinctively-sloping walls often three or four stories high, create an impression of modern antiquity. There's even an adobe Safeway supermarket. We strolled into the huge El Dorado Hotel, where earlier we had seen hotel staff throwing burning fireplace logs through a side door from a banquet-in-progress onto the street; evidently the flue didn't work. The hotel is gorgeously decorated, but Nanci overheard some guests saying they "needed to get their hoteling together."

It's wonderful to be in a city that's nearly 400 years old and so pleasing to the eye. There seems to be a group of quite wealthy inhabitants—the "filthy rich" somebody in town called them. I remember riding north out of town with Skip & Co. on a rural road that passed some opulent dwellings.

Something else I remember from that trip, and confirmed this year, is the large amount of broken glass along the highways in New Mexico. I considered sending a letter to Governor Tony Anaya about it, urging his support for a bottle bill. Fewer cans now that aluminum is being bought for recycling, but some of the shoulders are literally paved with shards of glass.

Finally, breakfast. Fresh fruit frappe, smoothed with cream, then orange slices with coconut, a basket of warm breads and pastries, then a "gepetto," their term for an omelette made in the waffle iron, and french toast stuffed with apples and nuts. All, of course, included with our room charge.

Following our leisurely meal we went to Base Camp for some gear purchases, then to other shops for gifts to send back home and to my sister Carol, who on May 1st gave birth to five-pound Rachel Sarah, my first niece of any weight whatsoever. Lunch was bean burritos at O.J. Sarah's, a little natural food cafe on Guadalupe. Good, but kind of expensive. Outside the wind was picking up.

We spent a fascinating two hours at the Museum of Fine Arts, a striking adobe building right on the plaza. Within was an exhibit of 20th-century drawings called "The Extended Line," featuring pen and ink, pencil, crayon, brush, and other media.

I realized I like the sparseness of information in line drawings and sketches—it draws me in, gives me room as a viewer to create, like short stories by Borges or music by Monk.

Bustling around the museum was a production crew working on a Friday morning live telecast for *Good Morning America*. Cables were stretched along the floor and nervous men with clipboards, cigarettes and walkie-talkies were pacing about.

Upstairs was an exhibit of colorful, primitive, and ritualistic Native American art from the collection of Dorothy Dunn, a schoolteacher who did much to encourage art education among the Indians. There were also pieces from the museum's permanent collection including works by Los Cinco Pintores, Sante Fe's first artists' group that flourished 1921-26. Will Shuster and Fremont Ellis were two members whose works were on display.

I had expected to see lots of Georgia O'Keeffe, but there were only one or two of her works. We strolled into the St. Francis Auditorium where a guard, who had seen Stravinsky playing the organ during a premiere of one of his works there, and asked "What's that?" to which Igor answered, "Bach" and the guard said "Who?" ("I almost got fired then," he said)—where this guard, I say, pointed to the six-foot tall murals along the walls depicting the life of St. Francis, patron saint of Sante Fe (which was once called "La Villa Real de San Francisco") and told us that O'Keeffe had wanted to paint those murals. When instead one Donald Beauregard got the commission, which he executed most of before dying in 1917, O'Keeffe conceived a lasting grudge against the state of New Mexico, which is why most of her paintings are in museums outside the state (I think there's a large collection somewhere in Minnesota). The museum here does have a few photographs, some by Steiglitz and some by Helen Laury, of O'Keeffe at various stages of her life.

We also entered an exhibit called "Personal Environments," featuring installations by five or six artists ranging from the abstract to the realistic and the surreal. One guy in his early 20s, Tim Prythero, had created incredibly detailed miniatures of Western scenes, such as a two-foot mobile home with bottle fence, and a dilapidated breadbox-sized Cactus Motel. Every paint flake, cigarette butt, smashed window, and faded detail is in place and perfect. It's a kind of amplified sight, whereby looking at the model you remember points you never noticed in the originals— an ennoblement of the totally ordinary. There was also one miniature by Roland Reiss, who gave a workshop at Sierra Nevada College last summer. His was an executive office scene with some symbolic elements—a can and paintbrush with red swatches painted on the floor, and a colorless man among the superrealistic, fully-colored men and women confronting each other.

I love museum gift shops. Great cards, always.

Back at Grant Corner, Komala made me a cup of tea and I wrote about

20 postcards. Then to our dinner at La Tertulia (Spanish for "the gathering place"). It's in a beautiful old convent building, once part of the Guadalupe Mission Church Complex on the historic Camino Real, the "Royal Highway" of the 16th and 17th-century Spanish conquistadors. Inside it feels like those days, with bare whitewashed walls and dark wood *vigas* (beams). Lots of little adjoining rooms, and very attentive service. We arrived a little early for our 8 p.m. reservation (procured a day in advance for us by our hosts) and I told the maitre d' that we'd wait in the lounge. "Oh, no, sir," he said. "We'll seat you in the living room." This was their waiting area, adjacent to an alcove full of religious artwork, images of saints, etc. Excellent margaritas.

How could we resist the paella? The waiter even swung by to show us the large iron platter, before returning to the kitchen to dish it out. Lots of seafood: shrimp, mussels, lobster, and two tiny Southwestern meatballs over saffron rice with vegetables. All good except the lobster, which was hard to extract from the shell and didn't have much of a flavor. But the price was unarguably low: $12.95 for each of us! Easily double that at a restaurant of comparable notoriety and atmosphere in California.

After dinner we strolled back to La Casa Sena to see if the piano player was still there. Instead, their entertainment was the bartenders and cocktail waitresses singing show tunes as they worked, including, when we looked in, "The Best of Times." Not them, but the wall of tobacco smoke, drove us back to Grant Corner, through a cold, light sprinkle.

May 8th   Day 22
65.6 miles
Sante Fe — Las Vegas, New Mexico

Our second breakfast at Grant Corner Inn consisted of the usual plus honeyed bananas rolled in crushed pecans and raisin-rice griddlecakes, sausage, and so forth. We saved the pastries for lunch later.

Outside it was quite chilly without much sun. A few snowflakes fell as we donned full armor, checked out, and rode the old Sante Fe-Las Vegas-Pecos Trail southeast out of town. The road paralleled the interstate for about 11 miles to Canarcito, where we got on it to cross Glorieta Pass (7432'), getting off at the Glorieta Convention Center only five miles later.

Glorieta is where the Confederacy was defeated in the Southwest, where General Canby's Federals were able to rout General Sibley's Texas volunteers when Colorado volunteers, based with Canby at Fort Union near Las Vegas, burnt the South's supply train. There's a Confederate memorial just south of Glorieta. A few days earlier, in Albuquerque, I saw a marker commemorating a repulse of the Union forces by a Confederate garrison there. Must have been previous to Glorieta. Our trail guide says that parts of *The Good, Bad, & Ugly* were based on this story.

This is now high pine country, at the southern tip of the Sangre de Cristo Range. Tall ponderosa pines among the juniper and piñon. The Pecos Wilderness area is nearby. Rather than mountains hereabout, the heights are mostly long mesas and ridges. Still pretty cold.

The Pecos National Monument is in the upper Pecos Valley past the little town of Pecos (sign: "Welcome to Pecos from Pecos Video"). Pecos was an important trading center for Indian and white alike. Situated on the divide between the Pecos and Rio Grande Valleys, between the mountains and the plains, it served as a contact point between the nomadic plains tribes and the industrious villagers along the Rio Grande. By the mid-15th century, immediately previous to the arrival of the strange bearded men in metal clothes from the South, they had concentrated themselves here in a multi-story, 650-room pueblo. Traders from the East were welcome for their goods—mostly buffalo hides—but suspect as to their motives and not allowed inside the pueblo complex after dark.

With the arrival of the Spaniards everything changed forever. Lured up from Mexico, Francisco Vasquez de Coronado took over Hawikuh Pueblo south of Gallup and sent out scouting parties to explore the region. People from Cicuye (Pecos) came to visit Coronado at Hawikuh bearing hides of a strange "humpbacked cow" (i.e., buffalo). Coronado sent Hernando de Alvarado, and the latter met at Pecos a Plains Indian who told of a rich land to the East called Quivira. The Indian returned to Coronado's new headquarters at the Rio Grande, and in the Spring of 1541 led the conquistadors as far, perhaps, as present-day Kansas, hoping they would die out on the plains. They soon tired of travelling the endless prairies, killed their guide, and returned to the Rio Grande country.

Other Spaniards followed, and by 1620 there was a full-fledged mission at Pecos. It was burned in the Pueblo Revolt of 1680, and a kiva built on part of its site. After the re-conquest another church was built, but by the end of the 18th century the Pecos population had dwindled due to disease—smallpox, introduced by the Europeans—and the eclipse of Pecos by the growth of greater trading centers, most notably Sante Fe. By the time the ruined church—its crumbling walls standing after their destruction much as we see them in 1986—served as a landmark along the Sante Fe Trail, it was deserted. In the early 1900s archaeologist A. V. Kidder began the excavations, using pottery styles as dating references, that would establish Pecos as an important ruin.

We walked around the trail, noting the great amount of unexcavated sites in the area. Good view up and down the Pecos Valley, and over at the wilderness area to the north. The Pecos Visitors Center, built only two years ago, is a marvelously beautiful structure of adobe and carved wooden beams—really first class. The bathrooms are all tile and woodwork; a far cry from the usual dingy, basic, government architecture!

From Pecos we rolled down the river valley for a while, as big black clouds gathered to the south. In the northern distance, it looked like it was snowing. We kept on 84/85 Alternate for awhile and just before we thought we had to rejoin the interstate, it snowed on us for a few minutes! During the brief flurry Nanci was accosted by ten dogs from an old house in the nearly-deserted hamlet of Rowe.

We followed a frontage road all the way to a KOA campground five miles south of Las Vegas, tipped off to its existence by Dale Bustamente at New Mexico Highlands University, buddy of my colleague Larry Mason. Larry thought Bustamente would have offered us free college housing, but he didn't.

Bob and Betty Sarr, our hosts at KOA, were witty and personable people from Ohio, who moved here to run the campground. People in Las Vegas, said Betty, were "old-fashioned enough to be friendly." Also, asked what the main industry of this town of 10,000 or so was, she replied, "Welfare."

People sometimes assume that because we're traveling on bicycles we're destitute. A fellow from Florida told me in the rest room that he and his wife had an old sleeping bag in their truck that we were welcome to use. I politely declined, and we spent the cold and windy night snug in our tent and zip-together bags beneath the juniper trees.

May 9th   Day 23
83.4 miles
Las Vegas — Conchas Lake, New Mexico

Next morning we packed up and headed into town for breakfast. Nanci had the first flat tire of the trip on I-25 just a few miles along, a rear tire that we patched and had rolling in no time.

Breakfast at the Hillcrest Restaurant, recommended by Betty, consisted for me of a green chile breakfast burrito, full of eggs and potatoes, while Nanci had huevos rancheros. Next to us some high school coaches drank coffee, smoked and talked, while a few old farmers jawed in the corner. On the way out I picked up a pamphlet put out by the church to promote Soil Conservation Week, and the new (?) "no-till" method, whereby crops are sown right over the stubble of last year's. This is meant to preserve the moisture in the soil.

We rode out of town past a natural foods store so we stocked up on Westbrae Ramen and other goodies. Old man came in sucking a cigar to buy a bottle of aloe. Outside we spoke to a young guy named Doug, who said his father, approaching 70, had ridden the U.S. in three stages on an old clunker bike. He investigated our equipment with interest.

Las Vegas ("The Meadows") has the slogan, "Where the Mountains Meet the Plains." It also has World College, based in an old castle which I hear was bought and heavily restored by industrialist Armand Hammer.

Also has authentic old Plaza Hotel, good place to stay, I heard, but we didn't even go and look at its supposedly beautiful exterior. Too itchy to get riding across what we knew would be a long dry haul to Conchas Lake.

Instead we rode out over what we thought would be the Plains forever. Rolling grasslands, gleaming in patches of sun, fences, occasional ranches, not much else. Huge dark clouds were dropping rain on all sides of us. Got hit by a few sideways spatters in the crosswind. Pulled on raingear, but no delivery. So we rode in and out of the wind, finally coming to a few short descents and then a turn to the south, right smack into the wind, at Trujillo—basically just a cluster of homes and a church. Then we curved back to the east, and suddenly before us, out of nowhere, was a 1600-foot descent in three miles down a steep bluff face, and around us towered mesas and hills in profusion. We were back in the mountains, at least for awhile. Some ponderosa pines here, too, in the shade of the steep rocky gullies. Otherwise just the usual "pygmy forests" of piñon and juniper. Once in awhile I catch the aroma of someone burning these woods—very aromatic, reminds me of campfires on the high plains of Arizona.

We rode along, learning from a roadside scenic marker that we were on the edge of the Canadian Escarpment, which borders the Great Plains. It was nearly 50 more miles, some of it steep or into the wind, to Conchas Dam and Lake. I got quite short-tempered for awhile there— guess I'm just tired of the headwinds, the ups and downs, the endless blank highway.

It's amazing, though, how much effect names have on my imagination. Here we are near the Canadian River, along the Canadian Escarpment, and all I can think of is pine forests and cool damp North Woods. Canada must be 2000 miles away at this point—the border, not even the pines. But it's a refreshing thought.

We rolled into Conchas—a reservoir built by the U.S. Army Corps of Engineers in the 30s—and were glad to set up our tent amidst the RVs, pickups and boat trailers at the South campground, a few hundred yards or more from the lake shore. In the distance, low mesas all around. Marginal restrooms with cold, push-button showers. I didn't take a shower and kind of regretted it because the washing really does seem to eliminate that pesky sleeping bag stickiness.

Talked to an old tattooed fellow for awhile, who had been camped there for three weeks. He said the wind had blown nearly every day. He fished for largemouth bass, walleye, pike, crappie, and chainsmoked Pall Malls. He also had boat trouble.

May 10th   Day 24 — Our 5th Wedding Anniversary
38.8 miles
Conchas Dam — Tucumcari, New Mexico

The next morning dawned clear, cloudless and windless—we heard our friend having more trouble with his boat. We struck camp quickly and headed for Conchas Lake Lodge for breakfast. They let us roll our bikes into the spacious lobby (doubles as a big polished-wood dance floor) and we went to a lakeview sunshine window for huevos with red chile (they were out of green). Leads me to wonder: how long will green chile last? Will it stop at the Texas border like the saguaro cactus stops at the California border?

Starting to hear more Texas accents too—they make two syllables out of one, like: "ey-ex-cent" for "accent."

Met some nice folks at the next table, Dr. Wayne Gares and his wife, administrators at Eastern New Mexico University in Portales. We got along fine, exchanged addresses. Wayne grew up in Tucumcari, and didn't have much to say for it. The main function of Tucumcari Mountain was as a landmark for westward travelers along this route. The town was a rail stop for the Sante Fe. We got a late start and rode the 32 miles there, going through some beautiful red clay deposits. Otherwise, very green short grass prairie, mesquite trees. Great wildflowers along the road right-of-way—yellow with purple, pink, white—it looks like someone spread a Meadow-in-a-Can along the shoulder.

Finally topped a rise—there were several—and saw Tucumcari Mt. We asked a cruising policeman where the Tucumcari Historical Museum was and rode straight there: three stories of junk with a nice, helpful white-haired lady in charge. Some of the things were old military uniforms, medical gear, black and white photos. Lots of the stuff used to be in the town drug store, Elk Drug. Lots of it fit the category "hadda be there"—i.e., even we couldn't flog up enough enthusiasm over it to stay too long. Not quite old enough or sorted right, or something. One whole room was full of brown rocks, containing "fossils" that were difficult to distinguish. Wise and witty sayings on cards, standing in frames like the sale signs above shirts in a department store, emerged here and there from the cluttered piles. $2.00 admission, but we got some pamphlets about Quay County, Tucumcari, and New Mexico out of it.

We also learned the "Ballad of Black Jack Ketchum," who was hanged here in 1901:

> In a wind-blistered cave out on Saddleback Mesa
> South from Tucumcari,
> Dirty, and mean as the Devil's eyes' gleam,
> Hid the posse's vulture-like quarry.
>
> He swooped down on trains
> Like blood flows through veins,
> And killed men—a dozen plus three.
> Till they dropped him a rope
> That ended his hopes
> Of going to hell in one piece.

(Black Jack Ketchum, it seems, was decapitated by the noose. There are black-and-white photographs of this scene on the museum wall.)

Tucumcari was born with the railroad in 1901. Ancient Tucumcari Lake was a watering hole for prehistoric animals and cave-dwelling *homo sapiens*, Spanish conquistadors, pioneers, outlaws, and trail riders of the Goodnight, Sante Fe and Comanchero trails which crossed here. The town was reputedly a pretty rough place then. "Where superhighways now rush, prehistoric man once hunted," states the caption on one modern postcard of busy Route 66.

After a stop at the ice cream store, we hightailed it to the Holiday Inn at the east end of town. Nanci put on her swimsuit and read *Shogun* by the pool while I sat in the room, watching *Star Trek* and writing in this journal. The Trek episode showed Captain Kirk on some desert planet making a cannon from a hollow tree trunk and freely-occurring diamonds (for ammo), sulfur, potassium nitrate, and coal (for gunpowder). His resourcefulness was inspirational.

So far on the trip I've been trying to find time to edit my journals into a series of articles to send to the newspaper back home. After spending most of several afternoons in a room, writing, I've decided I'll spend the time writing my journals and exploring, instead. The *Bonanza* readers will have to wait until our return.

The question of how far the green chile is to last is nearly answered. My dinner in the Holiday Inn consists of previously-frozen Mexican food and beer. Nanci has a steak. My combination plate is represented as including an enchilada in "green sauce," but it's nearly undetectable.

Chapter Three:
Climbing the Plains

May 11th Day 25
118.9 miles
Tucumcari, New Mexico — Amarillo, Texas

At breakfast they're out of milk, so no pancake batter, and the hot chocolate machine is broken so Nanci has to drink coffee. At 7 a.m. we're on the road to Amarillo.

Leaving Tucumcari was nearly flat, except for a few low bluffs about 10 miles out of town, and a couple of small rivers. We were waiting for the Caprock, the eroded edge of the high plains.

A good frontage road crossed from the south to the north side of I-40 at San Juan, New Mexico, 20 miles from Tucumcari, where there's a truck stop and free camping in a nice city park, although most of the rest of the town seems shut down, except for a motel and a few gas stations. Fat guy riding a little tractor tried to wave us a warning, but we didn't pay him any mind and continued through San Juan to a dead end. When we turned back to find the crossover, we got a taste of what it would have been like to ride westward today, heads lowered into the howling southwest wind.

The frontage road and a stiff tailwind take us the 40 miles to Endee, on the Texas border, where we stop for a juice break at a combination cafe and gift shop and chat with a nice old lady at the register. I had seen "Nemadsi pottery" advertised on a Stuckey's billboard and asked her what that was. Guy in the office behind her called out, "It's a Taiwanese tribe."

Over the past millions of years (we read from a roadside marker in San Juan), various mountains and seas have struggled for possession of the Southwest. Eroded debris from these mountains and sediments from these seas were washed over the plains, piling to incredible depths. Rivers cut some of it, but the main part sits high and dry as the Llano Estacado—the Staked Plains. The result is that we actually have to climb to get on the Plains.

Dr. Gares, back at Conchas Lake, had told us that no, I-40 didn't cross any caprock. But Mary Jo, our waitress at dinner in Tucumcari, said yes, the freeway just went right up it, whoosh!

Since estimates of road gradient by non-bikers are generally unreliable, we had no idea of what we faced. I had thought the little bluffs right after Tucumcari might have been it, for when we got to the top, nothing but huge rolling plains faced us, with long low mesas along the south. Far ahead, in the glare below the rising sun, I could see the twin ribbons of freeway perhaps rising slightly. So we beat it down the road, a tailwind (actually a starboard sternwind) pushing us at 15-20 mph along the smooth road. At the border, the little old lady at the cafe in Endee told us that the frontage road was good all the way to Amarillo "except up ahead where it goes through them hee-yulls." This turned out to be the real caprock, a long but steady low-grade climb for about a mile through pointy hills. Finally we were up on the Great Plains, riding across the Texas Panhandle, the "Golden Spread," towards Amarillo.

Crossing the border between New Mexico and Texas was rather like the change one senses between certain foreign countries. Suddenly, no more Rio Refulgio, Sangre de Cristo, or Gonzalez for Mayor. The names were now indisputably American: Deaf Smith County, Kline Ranch, Coldwater Cattle Co. Even in the cafes, groceries, and Dairy Queens we were patronizing, Hispanic faces were notably absent. And the roadside buildings, ranches, and irrigation gear seemed spiffier, more modern, and less like relics from the 19th century. I know that North Texas has history and is proud of it, but it's much less evident here than in ancient New Mexico.

Tucumcari Mt. had vanished rather sooner than we thought such an important landmark would—how did Coronado and his men, lured across the plains by their wily Indian guide, ever find their way back to the Rio Grande? The steady wind rippled the short grass like waves in the sea. If only the conquistadors had ridden bicycles, and had this Texas-sized bicycle path!

At Endee we enter Texas and the Central Time Zone, and have to get on the freeway for 20 miles to Adrian. It's not bad—a good smooth shoulder, and lots of new signs: DON'T MESS WITH TEXAS (anti-litter) and 72-OZ. STEAK FREE (if eaten in one hour) AT TEXAS STEAK HOUSE.

It's Texas's sesquicentennial and they're pretty high on themselves. A wagon train is slowly wending its way through the state, kicking off a round of commemorative events and parties wherever it stops. Some schoolchildren are also traveling with it, going to school on the road.

At Adrian we exit I-40 and ride past a Stuckey's, thinking to find a local cafe. But we ride by the inevitable grain elevator and a few closed stores before realizing it's Sunday, and Adrian is closed. A box of raisins each will have to suffice until the next town—Vega, 14 miles away.

The Texas Highway Department has furnished frequent rest stops by the roadside, either informal pullouts with litter barrels under the shade of tall old cottonwoods, or formal picnic areas with sheltered benches and tables. I think we've seen our last junipers and pines—even the trees northwest of Tucumcari were all mesquites.

Across the far grassy horizons only occasional clumps of trees are visible, with sometimes a house. Also silhouetted quite frequently against the clear blue sky are windmills, busy pumping water up from wells beneath, showing us the direction and velocity of the wind with their short blades high above the ground atop spindly scaffolding. Once in a while we see a modern one, a thin space-age trunk supporting a streamlined propeller. The towns, spaced closer and closer along the interstate, are first made visible to us by the tall grain elevators, two or more tank-like gray towers completely dominating the other single or double-story structures in town.

By now our tailwind has swung around, or the highway has, to give us a crosswind. It slows us down somewhat but not too badly. Coming into Amarillo, off to the right in a plowed field, is a row of red Cadillacs planted head-on, at an angle, about eight of them. This, I believe, is the "Cadillac Ranch" Bruce Springsteen sings of.

We've detoured from our Southwest Route map by taking I-40 out of Tucumcari instead of the indicated indirect south, east, then northeast route through Ragland and Hereford. So we're finding our way through west Amarillo on our own—the I-40 frontage road, now one-way on either side of the freeway, serves us well to a point. Look, honey, there's a Mervyn's! Maybe they're having a sale! Suddenly, in midturn, the road deadends at a railyard. We wander around a low-rent residential part of town, finding at last a road that underpasses the tracks a little to the south on 22nd Street, then north on Ross/Osage, and there's the Holiday Inn, framed by downtown buildings to the north.

This Holiday Inn is the swankiest so far, and the most expensive: $59.94 for two, king bed, including our 10% AAA discount. Next to the lobby is a dimly-lit chromium lounge and an enormous pleasure dome, or "Holidrome," with pool, billiards, ping-pong, even a miniature golf course. The restaurant's also the best of its kind so far, with a good salad bar and even sauteed vegetables and rice—just like home! After three beers and the 120 miles today I'm in no shape for anything but a look at the maps and bed. The air conditioner runs all night; this room, like the one in Tucumcari, has no ventilation other than the mechanical unit beneath the window.

Back in Tucumcari we had briefly considered diverting our course to Route 54, the Wichita road that slices directly northeast diagonally across the Panhandle. But from what we could tell, services looked slim, and as it turns out I'm glad we took the Amarillo way. Once in a while you need some of this corporate luxury.

May 12th   Day 26
51.5 miles
Amarillo — Lake Meredith, Texas (including a 10-mile detour to Alibates National Monument "Visitor Center")

Next morning there was a newspaper—the *Amarillo Daily News*, "The Morning Newspaper of the Golden Spread"—under the door, and I got coffee from the lobby and charted Holiday Inns across Illinois, Indiana, and Ohio while Nanci enjoyed her sleep-in.

A generous helping from the Cereal Bar, plus the usual eggs and pancakes, orange juice and coffee, and we're all set to roll 'em out the sliding glass door of the room, but ... I have a flat on my rear wheel.

It's evidently caused by a thorn, or as we've heard them called, a "Texas Tack." However it is a convenient place to patch the tire. I wash my hands four or five times—try doing *that* on the shoulder of the road!

I made telephone calls last night, since it was Mother's Day, and heard that the film I've been sending my brother Dick is badly overexposed—this from an automatic camera! I called Teresa Willis at the *North Lake Tahoe Bonanza* and yes, the Tri-X I've been sending her is the same way. Fiddlesticks. I stopped on the way out of Amarillo for new batteries and shot test rolls at different ASA settings, sending them to my correspondents for evaluation. It's kind of disheartening to learn that most of the Ektachrome I shot across the Southwest was wasted. Good thing I'm scribbling so much.

Headed over to Eastern Street, then North to 136, the Panhandle Boulevard, towards Fritch. It follows the elevated roadbed of the Wabash/Rock Island line for awhile, then veers north away from it. Soon we leave the flatlands and enter the rolling breaks of the Canadian River drainage. Bluffs off to the left. It's hot. Pretty good road, too, with wide, smooth shoulders. Like the rest of the Golden Spread west of Amarillo, it's cattle country with a little farming. We pass markers for the Sante Fe Trail, this branch of it first traveled by Sante Fe trader Josiah Gregg in 1840. Gregg annually carried $25,000 worth of goods to Sante Fe. This particular trail branch connected the river ports of Fort Smith and Van Buren, Arkansas, with the Southwest.

In 1849 a Captain Marcy of the U.S. Army made this branch of the trail famous when he guided a party of "respectable" citizens over it. Within a few months, goldseekers were following it to the California strikes. Over the years many military parties, trappers and hunters used it too. It was briefly considered as a route for the Transcontinental Railway, but the Civil War shifted sentiments away from the South, and a more northerly route was chosen. Here and there historical markers point out wagon ruts, still visible in the waving grass. Those were the days before barbed wire.

The plains have tilted on us, dipping in and out of various drainages. On the far left horizon the bluff-like shore of Lake Meredith is visible. Traffic is light—a few boats on trailers, a few trucks, the rest cars and pickups.

A few miles before Fritch, we come to the left-hand turn for Alibates National Monument and McBride Canyon. These are mentioned in our Southwest Trail book, and a compground is indicated at McBride. Plus, says the author, camping is allowed almost anywhere along the shore of the lake, a National Recreation Area.

We turn in toward the monument. On the way we learn from a marker that Dr. Charles Newton Gould, a paleontologist of the early 20th century, discovered the great helium gas wells of the Panhandle, biggest in the world (we saw Helium Road coming into Amarillo, but neglected to visit the International Helium Time Columns there). Gould also told drillers where to sink the first producing oil well in the Panhandle, and, more directly concerning the monument, he discovered fossils of Folsom Ice Age Man, 12,000 years old, in the flint quarries down at Alibates.

The pages of a garishly colored pornographic magazine fluttered in the hot breeze on the gravel around the marker. We rode on, mostly downhill, in a series of 90-degree turns through mesquite, on a road leading nowhere evident. About four miles in, there was a junction: left for McBride Canyon, right for Alibates. We curved to the right, steeply downhill, and at Mile 5 we came to the Visitor Center—a locked trailer with a sign: "Alibates Visitor Center—Guided Tours Only—Call for Reservations." No phone, no water, pit toilets, and plenty of biting flies.

We applied insect repellent for the first time on the road, sat down in the shade for a quick lunch, then rode out of that "hellhole," as Nanci called it.

Evidently there was lake access that way, since we saw a few cars come through, one with fishing poles. But we had little water, not enough to camp, and prospects of anything more than a primitive campground were slim. So we rode out the way we came, and another few miles uphill into Fritch, straight to the Dairy Queen.

This is our second Dairy Queen stop, and I think there's one in every small Texas town. We're getting hip to the world of Dilly Bars, Banana Blizzards, and Peanut Buster Parfaits. Soon I have three cups of different cold fluids before me: iced tea, water, and soda. The high school kids who ran the place were pretty indifferent, but we met some friendly folks: a prosperous-looking, well-groomed man, a younger man who we learned competes in triathlons, and a very wide black man, built like a football player.

"You look like long-distance bikers," the first man smiled. "I'll bet you couldn't wait till you got to Fritch!" They told us the easiest lake access for camping, just a few hundred yards south of the Dairy Queen, a turnoff labeled "Harbor Bay." A mile-and-a-half down, past some houses, was a good place to camp, on the flats among mesquite trees, right on the lake. We watched a beautiful sunset over the lake through the screened vent at the foot of the tent. It looked like a piece of art, hung on the tent wall. All was calm, peaceful, and for the first time since camping on this trip we ate a cold supper of fruit, bread, and cheese— no stove roar to shatter the evening stillness.

Over in one part of the camping area was what looked like a permanent site, occupied by a dilapidated green trailer, clothes hung out to dry on the bare trees. People drove through to fish and wade in the lake, and one fellow on a little motorbike stopped to chat, explaining that the only time he'd ridden a bike was when his driver's license had been suspended.

May 13th   Day 27
82.9 miles
Fritch — Perryton, Texas

Right before dawn, the wind came up—powerful gusts up to about 40 mph that flapped the tent walls (we hadn't put up the fly) and bent the flexible semi-circular poles into extended oblong shapes. I didn't think it would hold, but it did. When I got up, the skies were clear, although a definite haze (dust?) sat on the horizon, and the lake was whipped up into rows of waves. We packed and climbed out to the Dairy Queen for breakfast.

Like most Texas coffee shops, it was packed this morning (a Tuesday). I guess a lot of these guys in fertilizer caps, smoking and drinking bottomless cups of coffee, must have gotten up at 4 a.m. and already worked half a day. Else they don't do much. "Hey, Elon, whatcha doin'?" "Workin'." "I didn't ask whatcha s'pose' to be doin', I asked whatcha doin'?"

We're too far north here in Texas to see any armadillos, but we have seen snakes—mostly gold ones, crawling off the shoulder or squashed on the road. At Vega one old boy had a six-foot rattler in his pickup bed, and he pulled it out for everyone to see through the window while we were eating our Belt-Buster burgers. It was dead.

At the giant discount store where I went in Amarillo to get new batteries, the register at the camera counter was festooned with pictures of some frowzy women in smocks catching rattlesnakes out in the boondocks and putting them into burlap bags with long hooked sticks.

We enjoyed talking with so many people this morning that we didn't get off till 10 a.m. or so, riding north out of Fritch and circling around the northeast shore of Lake Meredith to Sanford (sign: "Hurry Back to SANFORD"—but why? there's not much there). Then we crossed the dam, learning it was built in the mid-60s by the Bureau of Reclamation (or, as one employee told me, by the Bureau of Wreck-the-Nation). Tall red banks reminded me in a way of Lake Powell, or Lake Mead. Much smaller, though, and red dirt rather than rock. Looked like some nice camping on the downstream side of the dam, by some swimming holes. We climbed out of, then descended back into, the Canadian River drainage, then out and up to Stinnett. Headwind the whole way, but we're still doing around 9-10 mph. Everywhere through this reddish, rocky land were gas rigs, rocker pumps, and big tanks, plus indications of subterranean high pressure pipelines (DANGER - POISON GAS). Refinery/storage facilities lined the horizon, and one gas flare. The whole place smelled like the kitchen when the pilots are out and spewing gas. We imagined we saw gas pouring out of vents in the earth—in one place there was a pool of crude by the road. Phillips Petroleum lease signs were hooked on the barbed-wire fences. The Amarillo paper reports that the Hughes Tool Company state rig count is 809—the lowest since 1943. Independent oilmen and Texas Governor Mark White are in Washington lobbying for an oil import tax to encourage domestic exploration. Dr. Charles Newton Gould, where are you now? He could just point and say, "Drill 'er here, boys" and it would be a gusher for sure.

It's rather arid in the breaks, with mostly mesquite growing. Back up by Stinnett, the fields begin to be cultivated again, as the land flattens out.

Stinnett, like Fritch, and no doubt Spearman and Perryton to come, are real friendly Texas towns. Everyone wants to know where we're from, where we're going, and what we do. And they all think they're the friendliest. "People here are *friendly*," they'll say.

It's a long, flat ride, with a few slight hills, past huge fields, with some cattle grazing here and there. A stiff headwind, actually coming in at about two o'clock on our starboard bow, slows us to 12-13 mph. I'm riding like Nanci now, trying to push the biggest gears possible. We're rolling in our noiseless, open-air vehicles across the fragrant Great Plains. There is a refreshing, refrigerant coolness in the air, like an ocean breeze.

We pass by a marker commemorating the two Battles of Adobe Walls. First one was in 1865, when 300 federal troops under Col. Kit Carson fought 3,000 Kiowa and Cherokee allies of the Confederacy. In spite of a brilliant defense, Carson lost. Later, in 1874, 29 buffalo hunters beat 300 of the same Indians, thus opening the Panhandle to white settlement.

The roads are mostly good, with wide shoulders. We cross from Hutchinson County into Hansford County and the shoulder became even better—wide and smooth. Hit the Pizza Hut in Spearman for dinner and phone calls. Friendly waitress told us we could probably camp in her parents' backyard. We decided, though, to try to make the 26 miles to Perryton by dark.

Well fed, we left not long after 6:30 p.m. and raced past Waka and Farnsworth, riding in the beautiful golden dusk. On the Western horizon, a huge black bank of clouds looked remarkably like mountains. It's dark when we ride into Perryton—"Wheatheart of the Nation."

Perryton is a big place for these parts—population 8,000—with the usual grain elevator, and a long commercial strip. We stop at a convenience store to ask directions, and I come out in time to rescue Nanci from an inbred weirdo with a huge hunk of chew in his mouth. "Pretty good pull from Fritch, even for a pickup," he drools.

We rode to the south end of town, along Route 83, the main drag, and stopped at the Ranchhouse Motel. It's operated by three really nice ladies from Iowa. One big room with queen bed is 25 bucks, which includes color TV and free coffee in the morning.

Later, looking for a beer, Nanci and I walk over to the Pizza Hut. No beer is served, and the young waitress with braces looks at us blankly when we ask where we can get one. Finally we're told by the clerk at an Allsup's convenience store that Ochiltree County is dry. Then why are so many pickups squealing down the street this evening? "Oh, that's kids," she said. "Drugs are real big here." I got a Hawaiian Punch and went back to the room to watch the weather, with which I am obsessed.

The commercials are for things like fertilizer and chewing tobacco: a clean young guy in a plaid shirt and overalls, working on his truck, looks up and pats first his bulging cheek, then the pouch in his shirt pocket. "Remember," he testifies with conviction, "if it hasn't got it *here,* then it doesn't go *here.*"

May 14th   Day 28
74.5 miles
Perryton, Texas — Meade Lake State Park, Kansas

Next morning over Perryton the sky was dark. We rode a little further south to the Ambassador Motel Coffee Shop for breakfast, then donned raingear for the 16-mile pedal to the next town, Bocker. Only a few spits here and there, but the clouds were threatening, with lightning bolts flickering all around. We had something of a tailwind, so we were making good time—about 15-18 mph. The country remains flat. "Drive friendly—it's the Texas Way."

North of Bocker we hit the Oklahoma border. This is the "panhandle," that strip of Oklahoma that gives the whole area its nickname. We learned from a carved stone monument that back in the mid-1800's this 34 x 167 mile region was known as No Man's Land, for when the Kansas border was set at 36°30' by the Missouri Compromise, and the Texas border by the Treaty with Mexico, this land was under no jurisdiction for a period of several decades at least, and became a refuge for thieves, rustlers, criminals on the run, and even some settlers. Eventually in 1890 it was incorporated into the Oklahoma Territory, which became a state in 1907.

We met a kid at a crossroads right north of the state line—he was on a BMX bike, what we used to call a Stingray, and asked the usual questions. He said his sister had bicycled here from Boston. Then he said, "Sure hope it rains." I understood what he meant. We both, in our opposite ways, were at the mercy of the weather. "It's been dry," he said. "Wheat's dyin."

As soon as we crossed into Oklahoma the nice wide Texas shoulder went away, and the land began to roll again. Texas is *so* well organized that every single road has a number, including four-digit numbers for the farm roads off the main routes. Some of them are even load-rated. In Oklahoma, this organization did not persist, and unmarked, unpaved roads went off in many directions.

A few sprinkles as we pulled into Beaver, Oklahoma, county seat of Beaver County, on the Beaver River (elsewhere called the N. Canadian). Beaver is also the site of the National Cowchip-Throwing Contest, held every year at the end of April. In the middle of town is a 12-foot statue of a grinning beaver holding a huge pasture pastry. Lunch at the Pizza Hut, where there were tons of school kids. They got out for the summer today!

Checked out Beaver State Park on the way out of town—big reddish sand dunes in one area, for use by off-road vehicles. Elsewhere there's a nice campsite by a tiny lake, but it might be a bit noisy if the dunes are busy.

Place names seem to have a great romantic attraction for me—hearing of the Canadian River in E. New Mexico, I dreamt of cool pines and shady lakes. Riding out of Perryton I saw signs to Darrouzett, and right away daydreamed we were riding through Southern Louisiana, my fantasy aided by the overall flatness and wetness of the land.

Another fantasy was triggered by the steady breeze, cool and zesty like the wind off the Pacific. I thought of our wonderful ride, this time two years ago, down the California coast.

The most shocking occurrence so far took place right after Beaver

State Park: we were riding along a flat stretch, into the usual wind, when I noticed a full-grown tan and black German shepherd at full speed on an intercept course. Not growling, but ears pinned back, teeth bared, just full-bore out to get us. "Better get a move on," I called to Nanci, riding in front, and I saw her start to shift gears. I would have passed her but for a light truck about to pass us. There seemed to be no hope— the dog, coming from the left, was nearly on us—when a car I hadn't seen whizzed by in the oncoming lane. With a loud, sick thunk the shepherd went off the car's bumper, pinwheeling into the ditch. Nobody stopped. We rode on in shock.

Soon we crossed the Kansas border, and after that the Cimarron River (I've always liked the Cimarron ever since Nanci, Skip, Diana and I rode along it from its source high in the mountains above Taos, through Angel Fire, and down the beautiful Cimarron Canyon to Cimarron, New Mexico three years ago). Although the yucca plant persists, sometimes in large spreads, it's definitely wetter around here. Grass grows wild. Wheat is dry-farmed more frequently, but there's still some big circular sprayer rigs for irrigation, and lonely well pumps, grinding away. Wheat in the non-irrigated fields looks a bit peaked, large swatches tending to brown. The fields look flat from a distance, but we're finding that there's plenty of hee-yulls, as the Texans say. Many fields tilt quite a bit, and are cultivated along the contour. Some fields haven't been planted yet, or have been very recently. One field full of shoots looked brown close-up, but shaded to deep green in the distance.

More trees are growing, too, and not just next to houses. Aside from a few bluffs, most of the watercourses have gentle, rounded banks.

We pulled into Meade Lake State Park with a deep black sky behind us. Paid the ranger $2, and he told us there were thunderstorm warnings up all around but none in the area. We pitched the tent in a sheltered spot right below the dam, on some grass and leaves beneath heavy tree cover, and walked halfway around the small lake for our pushbutton showers. The beautiful sunset over the lake reflected orange in the smooth water.

Skipping dinner, except for some trail mix, lemonade and a wheat roll, we retired, Nanci to sleep and me to write and listen to talk shows, news, and Nebraska weather on our pocket radio.

Later, we were alarmed to hear a scuffling and grunting over by our bikes, followed by scratching noises. After remaining inert for a while, hoping it would go away, I got dressed and reluctantly went out to find that a raccoon had torn a ragged, half-dollar size hole in my left front pannier, through which it was gorging on fruit bars and buckwheat ramen. About a foot of plastic bag protruded through the hole. I let out a stream of profanity, scaring away the coon, whose eyes glowed orange in my headlamp beam. I dumped the mashed remains into a trash barrel and, still cursing a blue streak, gathered up all our remaining food into two stuff sacks. It must have weighed 25 pounds. I tied the bags together and tried to swing them over a tree branch, succeeding only in pulverizing the contents of one bag. Finally I just took them into the tent, figuring a coon wouldn't be so bold as to invade our sanctum sanctorum. He wasn't, but we heard him out there awhile later, snuffling around. I had opened all the zippers on the packs, so he wouldn't tear into another one if he took a hankering to a bar of soap or something. I even worried about our shoes, since I had heard that coons liked to chew salty leather. So I went back out and brought those in too.

A little rain, but not much. Another thing about this campsite, nice as it was by the lake in the trees, was the drum concert. Now, it obviously wasn't anyone playing a drum all night long, but it sounded like it—a machine of some sort, rat-tat-tatting in a semi-regular pattern, over behind the park office at the east end of the lake. Never did find out what it was, and it stopped by morning. Neither of us slept real well.

May 15th   Day 29
60.1 miles
Meade Lake — Dodge City, Kansas

Next day was breezy and sunny, cool but warming up. Did the 13 miles into Meade in a headwind, after redistributing all the food and shaking the roly-poly bugs out of our shoes and clothing. Depending on the angle, the distant grain elevators that mark each town present different images—from giant fairy castles, to monolithic office buildings, to caped and hooded giants standing vigil over the wheat fields. Close up, they

---

look like missile silos. I had a grisly reminder of *The Day After,* while riding into Meade: a huge fan of contrails from the east, resembling the nuclear missiles launched near Lawrence, Kansas, in the television drama about World War III.

Meade was our first real Midwestern town: tall trees, wide streets, and the Lakewood Hotel on the corner, where we ate cheaply and well— beef tips (boiled to perfection) on noodles, mashed potatoes, peas, apple pie. For the women's room, Nanci took the elevator to the second floor; the men's room was in the basement, below the big lobby in this old brick building. Many senior citizens were lunching here, and everyone wanted to know the usual where's and when's, including one tattooed guy in a white short-sleeved dress shirt, who was about to tour the U.S. in his camper. "We're taking Route 23 out of town," I told him. "Oh, 83?" he said; then, seeing I was confused, added, "I was born and raised here, and I'll always call it 83."

Beautiful day, but no time to check out the Dalton Gang hideout—a house on a hill with a tunnel to a nearby barn—or the county's High Plains Museum. We still have 45 miles to Dodge City, so we got underway. Absolutely no one on 23, but the road's in terrible shape. 56 was better, but much busier. Came into Dodge with a stiff crosswind from the southeast, turned north on 50/56 and found the Water Sports campground just a mile up on the right. Grassy campsites on the lake beneath trees, run by very friendly people. We paid $8, took showers, did laundry, set up the tent and wiped it clean, reveling in the breeze and hot sun, then walked a mile downtown to dinner. From among the many fast-food outlets we chose a Golden Corral steakhouse, which was really good, not so much because of the meat ("Cut fresh every day, never frozen") but the huge salad bar and baked potato bar.

Next to us were six Mennonites, three men and three women seated across from each other. Men in beards, clean lips, Western attire (white shirts, tooled leather belts, boots), and women in pink dresses and black skullcaps. Nanci walked by in her short shorts toward the salad bar, and I could swear I heard the words "daughter of Satan." "Thanks for dinner, Ivan," said one of the women later.

The waitresses at the Golden Corral treated the Mennonite party with extra care, and well they might—it was German Mennonites from Russia who introduced Turkey Red, a hard red winter wheat, to Kansas in 1874.

Afterwards we went on a walking tour of Dodge. Boot Hill was locked up, but we peered through a crack in the fence at the graves of one woman and 27 men, buried with their boots on or behind their heads. Nearby stood a monument to Wyatt Earp, who was hired in 1876 to bring law and order to Dodge, and did so within two years. Also a statue commemorating the cowboy: "On the ashes of my campfire this city is built," reads the legend, and there's even a big statue of a steer, acknowledging that it was the cattle drives in the 1870s that built Dodge, eleven years during which five million head were driven to the Sante Fe trailhead here.

"Dollar a day, cold biscuits, gravy and lots of beans—only good men need apply," read an old advertisement for men to work the longhorn drive. Most of the newcomers ended up "riding drag"—i.e., eating dust behind the herd.

Dodge began in 1872 as supply center for buffalo hunters busy eradicating the giant herds, partly for robes and bones for bone china, and partly because the U.S. Army wanted to weaken Plains Indians by removing their single most important source of food and raw materials.

We walked up "Gospel Hill" to see three old churches, including a 1898 Episcopal Church of native sandstone. The Carnegie Library, built with funds from the steel magnate, is a round brick building. It's been restored into a community art center. We saw the "Home of Stone," also of native limestone, built in 1879. We walked along Matt Dillon Street, Gunsmoke Avenue and Wyatt Earp Boulevard.

We walked back by the park, its roads full of screeching cars. The Lone Sentinel marker indicates the place where a tree stood to mark the ford across the Arkansas River for pioneers. The river is dry now, and they wouldn't need a ford. We walked past, of all things, a Vietnamese pool parlor (one of two in town!).

If I were hired today to bring order to Dodge, I'd start by enforcing the speed laws. "Drive Drunk—It's the Kansas Way."

May 16th   Day 30
62.6 miles
Dodge City — Larned, Kansas

Next morning we had one of the worst breakfasts to date at a little storefront cafe which, according to our campsite host, was open only when the retired couple that ran it didn't feel too ill to work.

Leaving Dodge, there's a "Scenic Viewpoint," which happens to be above a huge feedlot. We learned that Dodge has the capacity to host 45,000 feeder cattle per year. They take them in at 600-700 pounds, and add 400-500 pounds to them before shipping them off to the meat market, where an 1100-pound cow is good for about 600 pounds of meat. It smells pretty gamy.

The route out of Dodge follows the Sante Fe Trail, since 1880 the route of the Atchinson, Topeka, & Sante Fe Railroad. The railroad was the reason many of these towns, including Dodge City, got going in the first place. I imagined a cowboy's growl: "Rode into Dodge. They had a few troublemakers there, so we cleaned the place up. Now it's quiet. Too quiet. I don't like it." So we hit the Sante Fe Trail.

Highway 50/56 out of Dodge was terrible for awhile, with lots of truck traffic and no shoulder. We had a tailwind, though, and averaged 15-18 mph. Soon we regained a shoulder, and rode a rapid 38 miles to Kinsley, where we toured the Edwards County Museum, which includes a sod house with authentic furnishings, dating from 1870-1890 when the Plains Indians were being booted off the land. The exhibits are in good condition here, including some Springfield rifles and Colt revolvers. An old man in white shirt, suspenders, and bow tie was in attendance; he just sat there, or stared out the glass door.

There's a big signpost in Kinsley, with two big white wooden arrows. One says,   SAN FRANCISCO - 1561 MILES   and the other,   NEW YORK - 1561 MILES.   The halfway point, maybe, but not for us. We've 1764 miles on the old cyclometer so far, only about two-fifths of the entire trip.

We crossed the Chisholm Trail, along which cattle were driven from Texas to Abilene, Kansas. Wheat still grows everywhere, but also corn, soybeans, sorghum. Farm traffic, trailers, pickups, backhoes, cattle trucks.

Plenty of trucks. Big ones.

We lost the shoulder after Kinsley, and gained a headwind of increasing intensity. By Garfield, 11 miles out of Larned, the 40 mph gusts were blowing me off the road into the (thankfully) grassy hardpack by the side of the pavement. I have been told that this is the heart of sandbur country, scattered with little multi-pointed devils as deadly as ninja throwing stars. At least one of our two flats thus far is from them, I believe.

Fought our way to Larned at 7-8 mph, with some intermittent windbreaks from clumps of trees. There's no shoulder until right before town. Found the Locker Room, the local bike shop taking up part of Bailey's Decorating Center on the main drag of this medium-sized small town. It's open and the owner, Bert, is very helpful, as was the young woman in the street who pointed him out. Bert sold Nanci a pair of Spenco gloves and a bike cover, and gave us a new route out of town to avoid a section of Highway 19 that is now gravel. This is where the Southwest Bike Trail ends, connecting with the TransAmerica trail that runs from Astoria, Oregon to Yorktown, Virginia. We'll follow it as far as the Great River Route in Missouri.

Now we're in the local Best Western, on the north side of town where all the lodging and cafes are located, and we're glad, for even though it cost us $32, outside it's rainy, windy, and very chilly.

May 17th   Day 31
76.7 miles
Larned — Hutchinson, Kansas

Rocker-type oil wells, seen since west of Amarillo, and thickly through the Texas-Oklahoma area, are still present here in Eastern Kansas but diminishing in number. These old black tarry tanks with their ancient pipes and fixtures contrast with the gleaming new equipment and pumping stations we saw near Lake Meredith. We've finally stopped seeing "Coronado passed by here" markers—the last one was in Dodge City, where they claim he crossed the 100th meridian along the Arkansas

River there (native Kansans call it the "Ar-KAN-sas"). How did the Spanish explorers, following a treacherous Indian guide across these featureless plains, encased in heavy iron armor in the dead of summer, ever find their way back to New Mexico?

The 100th meridian, bisecting Kansas, is considered a dividing line between the arid higher plains and the more humid lowlands. Every day we're seeing more trees, and the fields are getting smaller.

Wind and rain all last night in Larned, and this morning it's still grey and windy but no more rain. On the road after breakfast at the Dan-Do Cafe we're still fighting the wind from the north, but doing about 10-11 mph. The roads run at perfect right angles to each other through these flatlands, enclosing regular sections of one square mile.

(A note to those who follow: Eastbound, KS 19 is no longer paved beyond U.S. 281, toward the Quivira National Waterfowl Refuge. You need to cut south on 281 four miles, then turn left, and ride five miles to Hudson. There the JJ Cafe is a great place to stop and you can camp in the park. Hudson is a very small, tree-shaded town with a flour mill and nearby oil rigs. Then jog south again three and one-third miles past Hudson, and take a left about four miles south, toward Hutchinson. They say 19 will be paved again someday. Maybe not, though, if the waterfowl have their way.)

Ever since Texas they've been baling hay in huge rolls, maybe 5'x5', like giant toilet paper. Today we saw some bigger stacks, like big bread loaves.

Sunflowers are not yet numerous here in the Sunflower State but they do occur alongside the road. It's fun examining the roadside trash as we near a town, to find out what kind of fast foods are there, and what kind of beer they drink. People have been asking us, "What are you doing this for—a cause or something?" Now we have one: the 4-D Boosters—Discourage Disposable Diaper Dumping.

I never heard of this use of the word "abstract" before, as in signs on certain homes by the road: "Fast, Efficient, Confidential—Bonded ABSTRACTORS." This is short for "abstract of title," a brief history of the ownership of a piece of real estate. Land is all there is around here: the name of the Larned paper is the *Tiller & Toiler*. We ride past fields waiting patiently beneath the changeable sky.

We got into Hutchinson, a pretty big town of about 40,000, in time for dinner. We'd fought a northeast wind all day, and after 77 miles we were bushed. Burgers at Dake's, after a brief consideration of Burger King across the street; but we can go to one of those anywhere. The wind didn't let up, so we decided to call it quits and check into the Holiday Inn. The $62 charge was a little steep, but it was first-class, with "Holidrome" facilities, a jacuzzi, and free movies on the TV. Due to an abundance of families with kids, the place was a screaming madhouse. So after a brief soak we retired to our room and watched *The Adventures of Buckaroo Banzai Across the 8th Dimension.*

May 18th Day 32
110.8 miles
Hutchinson — Eureka, Kansas

Next morning after some blueberry pancakes we're off, taking a back way down to US 50 by the airport. This is the same highway, I'm happily homesick to realize, that runs back across Colorado, Utah, Nevada, along the east and south shores of Lake Tahoe, and down to Placerville and Sacramento. The wind isn't as bad, there's some sun, and we ride 30 miles to Newton. Sunday morning means nearly everything's closed, but at 11 a.m. a Bonanza Steak House opens and we eat lunch.

Newton is where the Mennonites moved in 1873 from Southern Russia, where they had been invited by Catherine the Great to escape persecution in Europe. They had made the southern steppes a major wheat-producing region, and proceeded to do the same with central Kansas, bringing their hard winter wheat and establishing mills to grind it. Although they do follow certain customs of dress and grooming (see Dodge City), they drive late-model cars and the farms are fully mechanized. Churches are everywhere.

After Newton the country opened up again; we felt as if we were on the edge of the plains near Dodge City again. Rolling fields stretched to the horizon. Cattle were more frequent, and we began to climb some low hills.

The little town of Cassoday—"Prairie Chicken Capital of the World"—is barely an interchange on the Kansas Turnpike. Everything's closed except the run-down little wooden gas station where a couple teenagers are working on a big-tired Firebird. We picnic in the grass down an unpaved side street, eating leftover bacon from the Dan-Do Cafe, and then ride some narrow farm roads, turning alternately 90 degrees left and right in and out of the wind, to US 54 at Rosalia (only a post office and grocery). This is a major road out of the Wichita area, with fast trucks, freeway-sized gravel shoulders, and at least an inch-high dropoff from the pavement. We fear for our lives.

Nevertheless, the scenery is inspiring. Low sun at our backs is illuminating the rolling Flint Hills (part of the Bluestem Pasturelands) and it's a gauzy, idyllic landscape, with woods, small lakes, and the first vistas we've seen for quite awhile, as we crest each of the long, low hills. Despite the resumed easterly direction (we had flown south for awhile ahead of the wind), progress feels easier—maybe the wind is dying. The traffic thins out some, and soon we're in Eureka, riding between trees over a stone bridge downstream from some falls, looking to take advantage of the town's hospitality.

The city park looks green and inviting this late in the day, with water, restrooms and picnic tables, but Nanci is coming down with a sore throat, so after briefly inspecting a run-down truck stop motel, we settle on the Blue Stem Lodge for $28. Our fourth dinner at a Pizza Hut, then TV in the room. I'm tired.

I got a kick out of one TV commercial between scenes of *On the Wings of Eagles*. Using graphics usually reserved for pimple creams or pain relievers, the announcer sings the praises of some weed-spraying equipment: "It goes deep, to get them where they sleep, and all without additional tilling!" Cut to two guys in plaid shirts, sipping coffee (in the Dairy Queen at 9 a.m.?), sounding like housewives confidentially discussing laundry detergents and their husbands' shirts, one saying, "Without tilling, Frank. You know what that means?" "Yeah," Frank says thoughtfully, "more moisture. No more weeds, and more moisture—I could get used to that," like he was saying, "Headache's gone—and no upset stomach!"

May 19th   Day 33
65 miles
Eureka — Chanute, Kansas

Next morning we backtracked a mile into town to eat at the City Cafe. We sat next to white-haired Pearl, the former cook here (sign over door says "Pearl's Kitchen"), who is on her third knee implant and sits, eats her oatmeal, and chats with the townspeople; she's been in the restaurant business since she was 15. "I don't know anything else," she tells us quaveringly.

One local old guy told us of seeing 1200 cyclists coming through in 1976, the inaugural year of Bikecentennial's TransAmerica Trail; they put them up overnight in town, and cussed them the next day on the road.

Although it lacks paved shoulders, Highway 54 is not too bad to the Toronto Lake turnoff. It's another beautiful, cloudless day, and we're riding through the Bluestem Pasture, named after the grass that grows hereabouts. It's a remnant of the prairie that once stretched from the Eastern forests to the High Plains. This region forms a huge oval running northwest to southeast, several million acres in two counties. This particular county, Greenwood, in an average year has more cattle shipped in to fatten at pasture than were driven to all the towns in Kansas during any year of the wild Texas cattle drives, 1866-1885.

But we see less and less cattle along our route, and fewer pumpjacks (the rocking oil pumps—evidently the tin drummer at Meade Lake State Park). The fields continue shrinking, and the hills are getting steeper. I can't believe we haven't been rained on yet—there's water lying in all the unplowed, unplanted fields, and the rivers and creeks are running full and muddy brown.

Our route seemed to indicate we were to follow Route 105 past Toronto Lake State Park, but 105 turned *into* the park. It was the wrong way, but we got to ride across the dam, look at the lake, and talk with the friendly, funny women at the park office. We talked about how the pumpjacks were located in peculiar patterns, only in certain places, and that over here they only needed to go down 500-600 feet for oil, while fifty miles west they had to go down a thousand. They also spoke of water witching, using a peach sapling for a divining rod.

More county roads, and hills, to Chanute. Some of the road surfaces are pretty bad, which slows us down. The turn at Roper is somewhat unclear; even the town is unsigned. But we find our road—old Highway 39—at a ruined Chamber of Commerce building. Wild roses line the road, and some squashed turtles and coons. We've only done 70 miles and I feel like a hundred (miles or years, take your pick). 99-cent roast beef sandwiches at Hardee's taste pretty good, and while I write, Nanci walks to the Walmart for a 40-pound sack of groceries.

Chanute gets its name from Octave Chanute, born in Paris in 1832 and later chief engineer for the Leavenworth, Lawrence, & Galveston Railroad. His experiments with primitive hang gliders predated the Wright Brothers' work at Kitty Hawk. Many of these eastern Kansas towns got their start from antebellum settlers coming in to try and sway the new state to one side or other on the slavery question. The fanatic abolitionist and eventual hero of the north, John Brown, was an early Kansas farmer who began staging bloody border raids on pro-slavery Missouri.

We settled at the Safari Campground, on the edge of the City Park south of town between the golf course and baseball diamonds. It's free. That evening we met Tom, who is cycling east to west on the TransAmerica. He's a quiet, serious guy, who seems young to have already been in the Army like he says. He's headed for Evergreen State College in Washington state, near where he grew up in Bellevue. Tom told us about some features of the trail ahead including bad roads in Missouri, Lazy Louie's near Marshfield, and the Rayfield Hotel in Eminence.

I walked a long way from the park to buy a beer, and the lady at the convenience store wouldn't sell me two bottles, so I had to get a quart or a six-pack. Crazy Kansas liquor laws. Also noticed that the liquor stores all look the same: nothing but a small neon sign reading "Retail Liquor Store." But in the Pizza Hut in Larned, the waitress couldn't sell us a pitcher because "there was only two of us"; we had to each buy a glass. And in Eureka, no beer was served at the Pizza Hut on Sundays.

Chapter Four:
Aux Arcs

May 20th   Day 34
92.6 miles
Chanute, Kansas — Golden City, Missouri

Everything was soaked with dew in the morning. We made corn chowder for breakfast, then rode south and east over the Neosho River toward Girard. Here on the Neosho was a mission founded in 1824 to serve the Osage Indians, who were gradually being pushed westward. The Indian agent and some of the chiefs didn't like the mission, though, and according to the historical marker "Indian rowdies" often disturbed religious services. The mission closed a few years later, and the Indians signed a treaty agreeing to a reduction in their reserve. A few years later they were shipped to Oklahoma—chiefs, rowdies and all.

Looks like a nice camp/roadside rest at Shaw; the sign says it was closed by the state of Kansas in 1982 but subsequently renovated and kept up by the Erie Golf Club.

A few hills on the way to Golden City but nothing severe yet. Although we're still seeing cattle, there are as many dairy cows, and hogs are starting to appear, muddy to a line along their flanks, obscenely pink elsewhere. Lots of alfalfa being cut and baled. As we slowly attain higher ground, the big muddy ponds are starting to disappear, and it's incredibly green everywhere. A few spits of rain as we pull into Golden City.

Kansas had been so friendly that I suspected Missouri would suddenly shock us with indifference or downright hostility. But crossing the state line was nothing special. A few miles before we'd ridden through Pittsburg, Kansas, a former frontier town. Some big old stone buildings along Broadway, the main street. We'd come into town via a side road, the directions for which on the Bikecentennial map read: "Third paved road to the left, by a power pole marked K4601 KG&E." I drank coffee and wrote cards in the Mr. Quick burger stand while Nanci made her weekly call into work. Mr. Quick was a friendly place—they said other bikers had been through. It was actually the only restaurant we saw except for a Dairy Queen off route to the north. Strange for a town of 10,000.

Riding into little Golden City we saw a couple of loaded touring bikes parked outside the Mayfair Cafe. We rode through town and made camp in the city park, a nice place with a covered picnic pavilion, restrooms, cold showers and electric lights. I walked back into town for a small milk-to-go in a styrofoam cup, an essential ingredient for our powdered soup mix, and saw one biker gorging himself at the Mayfair's $4.25 all-you-can-eat buffet, while the other was in the phone booth talking rapidly. Later they came over to camp and we met Jeff, on a seven-month leave from IBM, and Tim, a fast-talking professional cyclotourist. They're on a seven-month tour, designed by Tim, from their home in Poughkeepsie, New York, down to the Bikecentennial Route, across to Kansas, then down the Southwest Trail to San Diego, then up the coast, inland at Crescent City, over to Bend via Crater Lake, then back on the Bikecentennial trail, cutting south through Texas (via Amarillo & Lubbock), Mississippi, Alabama, Louisiana, and ending in Florida in

November.

Tim was one of those guys who never quite listens to what you say, and has biked everywhere you have. He carried a tape recorder in his handlebar bag, to record his comments. I think Jeff was a little tired of him already—they didn't seem to ride together at all, and were pretty self-sufficient, i.e., no shared equipment. Tim had the skinniest legs of any biker I've ever seen; whereas Jeff, on the other hand, was beefier and started the day, as we discovered, with calisthenics. Both of them decided to sack out on picnic tables beneath the pavilion.

May 21st   Day 35
83.8 miles
Golden City — Marshfield, Missouri

At breakfast we met a guy in the cafe who said he'd often thought of riding a bike across the country; he was a small guy, round head, white fringe and moustache. He said, "Well, I've got an artificial limb now," pointing to his leg. I told him, "Go ahead." "I just might," he said.

The hills began for real today. As we climbed into the edge of the Ozark Highlands, the streams turned clear as their beds became pebbly. It was a roller-coaster ride up and down, very steeply, across streams and small rivers. "Impassable During High Water" is a common sign, and the low creek bridges have gauges next to them so you can see how far under water they are in flood season: one, two, or three feet.

Passing through towns called Ash Grove, Walnut Grove, and Fairgrove, and the stands of hardwood trees are evident everywhere. In fact, Ash Grove bills itself "The Home of the Ash Tree." Smells of honeysuckle, new-mown hay, and death are intermingled, the last from a plentitude of squashed turtles and possums.

In Ash Grove we're served one of the noontime country dinners we're getting used to: roast beef, chicken, or breaded pork chop with mashed potato or "jojo" (baked potato quartered and deep fried), salad, vegetable, rolls, and pie. All for an incredibly low price: $3, usually. The cafes where we take our lunch break are hotbeds of cronyism—everybody knows everyone else, the old guys in overalls drinking coffee and discussing crops and the weather, while the professionals, in lighter shades of collar, are also eating lunch—the bank employees, firemen, building inspectors, and so forth.

Turns out our day will be 80+ instead of 75 miles as originally estimated. These hee-yulls are something; they tire us out, though we maintain an average speed of 10 mph, the five mph ascents being offset by hurtling descents at 30-35 mph.

We were amused to notice quite a few tractor-trailers on the road through here with "Truck Driver School" and "Student Driver" painted on the side.

Rolled into Marshfield, and reading the marker in front of the courthouse learned that this is the county seat of Webster County, named after Daniel Webster, born in the town of Marshfield, Massachusetts. At 1480 feet it's the highest county seat in Missouri, founded in 1824 by settlers from Tennessee and Kentucky, later the scene of several Civil War skirmishes. The town gained some notoriety from the song "Marshfield Tornado" by bluesman Blind Boone, about an early 20th-century twister that killed 65 and caused $1,000,000 in damages.

I had called City Hall from our lunch stop at Ash Grove, and a harumphing, friendly man told me it was okay to camp at the city park. "Have fun," he said. The park, on the north side of town, was expansive but had no unlocked restrooms or showers except for a trashed men's room over by an unoccupied farmers' market arcade. Also some covered picnic pavilions. After a thorough scouting of the thickly wooded area we camped next to but out of sight of the road that came down steeply from town, by a stream near a picnic table with a water spigot. The park is very green, with flowering trees.

We cooked soup and ate sandwiches in the dark, hung our food as a precaution against varmints, and sacked out. In order to eliminate sleeping-bag stickiness, we'd learned to shower before retiring. Nanci took a cold sponge bath at a faucet near our campsite; I grumpily refused, and suffered for it.

May 22nd   Day 36
61.5 miles
Marshfield — Houston, Missouri

Next morning it was cloudy, with wind. We rode back up to the town square and ate at Swain's Cafe, a typical greasy spoon. Some friendly redneck farmers outside gave us directions, and we hit the road. Just outside of town the wind turned from the south-southeast, and it began to rain. Our first liquid precipitation. We suited up, but it didn't last very long.

Rode by Lazy Louie's Bicycle Camp without stopping. It was a small house alongside a few slightly larger barn-like buildings in a compound set into the trees. We'd heard from Tim that Louie charged $1/night, and had bike parts for sale and tools to loan. Tim said he was treated to a few meals, but hadn't liked Louie: "Oh, he's always trying to sell me something."

At lunch in Hartville the sun was practically out. We devoured big country dinners with good cherry pie for dessert. Old black guy in cafe, joking with other good old white boys in a raspy Amos-and-Andy voice.

The country around here, on the Ozark divide between the Arkansas and Missouri River drainages, is noted for fruit and poultry production. We're passing lots of dairy farms, too. So why do we get only non-dairy creamer and margarine? Economics, I suppose. Like a Third World country that exports all its products. Or maybe it's the heat.

The going is fairly level to Houston, seat of Texas County (biggest in Missouri). Little bit of rain and some rush hour traffic as we get into town. First motel on the right is the Lazy L (no relation to Louie), where I plunk down $21.15 for a big double out back with TV and bathtub. Clean mom-and-pop-type place; next door is the Lazy L Cafe. What else do we need? Nanci went to do laundry while I goofed off in the tub. Dinner at the cafe was chopped steak and Texas toast.

May 23rd   Day 37
41.7 miles
Houston — Eminence, Missouri

Today it was raining with some thunder. By the time we were on the road, after a Lazy L breakfast, it had stopped. Not too hilly yet, even fewer cattle and almost no farms—just deep woods. The term "Ozark" may be from "Aux Arcs" — "in the country of the Arkansas." The region is one big plateau, very old as mountains go. Flowing water has deeply creased the soft limestone and dolomite that overlies a granite core. Maximum elevation is under 2000 feet—well worn down, I imagine, from its ancient height.

Last night during our Lazy L dinner we heard Hoyt Axton on the radio between innings of the Kansas City Royals game, pitching Busch beer to Ozark listeners: "I was hiking out by Lake of the Ozarks . . . provisioned at Osage Beach . . . 10 cases of Busch and 300 pounds ice." His voice reminded me of Tahoe City, but I found it hard to imagine such a comfortable fellow backpacking, let alone with such a load. The next day we saw plenty of Busch cans along the roadside.

Today I was riding behind Nanci when I came round a bend and saw her stopped and conversing with a woman in a blue van. Her name turned out to be Phyllis, her game snagging bicyclists for social purposes. She's going shopping in Houston but her husband Peter, an Englishman, is home and expecting to entertain all passing cyclists. Sounds good. We proceed, and meet a westbound cyclist just before Summerville, who tips us off to watch for a quilted scarecrow couple, seated on a bench by the road, with the man's arm waving a white handkerchief. It's rigged to a line coming from the porch, where Peter, a bald, bearded, slightly paunchy but very cheerful guy in rubber boots is pulling it. They're flying a hybrid Union Jack/Stars and Stripes above the Jolly Roger. He welcomes us in and lays on homemade shortbread, chocolate chip bars, tea, and the best coffee I've had since leaving home. Delightful conversation in the parlor, adorned with quilts and needlework, well-strewn with piles of *New Yorkers*. They keep a log, in which we're numbers seven and eight this year, with 60-75 signed in from last year, mostly during July and August. Piles of cards and letters from those folks, from all over the U.S. and Europe.

"I never go anywhere," says Peter. Talkative Phyllis, who we didn't remain long enough to see again, does the shopping, but even she hasn't been farther east than Eminence. She's a transplanted Northern Californian, and she and Peter met in a bar at 1 a.m. in Elk, on the North Coast. They seemed a little Bohemian for this region. "Fortunately," said Peter, "we have some money." His folks are farmers in Norfolk, Great Britain, growing seeds and breeding hogs. Peter also talked at some length about Brawley, California, down in the Imperial Valley. He used to live there, and says that the median per capita income is six figures, concentrated in the Anglo population, who are 15 percent of the total. Says it's a hub of the rich and famous—Jerry Brown, Gerald Ford—and we rode right by it! Somehow I can't picture Robin Leach out there with the RVs and ATCs.

We leave two hours later—"We will probably never see each other again," Peter says cheerfully—but there's plenty of other people in Missouri, and down the road in Summerville I talk with venerable old Lloyd Mitchell, Texas County sheriff's deputy and southern gentleman. He tells me that the season is advanced two or three weeks this year, and in any case it's a good thing we're not coming through in July or August.

Further on we find another westbound biker, an energetic retired man going from Harrisburg, Pennsylvania, to visit his Coast Guard son in Seattle, and perhaps ride the California coast with him. Gave us some info about conditions ahead for us, and we told him about the Quivira detour. In Chester, Illinois, on the other side of the Mississippi, he'd run into a bank and emerged to find his cyclometer surgically removed—wiring, sensors and all—from his bike. Nothing else disturbed. He'd also ridden through some brief but quite heavy rain.

A few miles later (good thing we'd planned a short day today!) we halt to climb a fire lookout tower. Far above the pines and hardwoods, we emerge to see rows of ridges, gray in the fog and humidity, in every direction. Far off to the east there are a few higher knobs, barely distinguishable in the haze.

Soon we plunge into Alley Springs, and take lunch at a picnic table by the clear flowing stream, up from an old mill that Nanci's visiting while I sit here on guard duty, writing. The clouds have broken, and the sun is warming things right up, though the intense heat is relieved slightly by a five-mph breeze. This is Jack's Fork of the Current River, which emerges from a nearby hole in the ground. The limestone that makes up a good deal of the Ozarks is permeated throughout with water—there's hundreds of springs around, including many circular, spring-fed ponds on the land we pass. Alley Springs here has an average flow of 65 million gallons. Down by a red mill building, from a big limestone hole, flows all this clear, glacier-blue water, gushing through the open wooden gate of the mill to instantly create a river, floated on by thousands of canoeists and inner-tubers each season—part of the Ozark National Scenic Riverways.

Out of Alley Springs is the first really steep hill—only a half-mile long, so not as bad as it could be. But I'm still in my lowest gear, and out of the saddle, standing on the pedals all the way up. Threatening clouds gather as we roll into Eminence's narrow streets, surrounded by high wooded ridges. We rent a cubicle in the Rayfield Hotel for $13, bath down the hall. Reminds me of the Ouray Hotel in Colorado. We're really crammed into this tiny room: two bikes, our gear, a dresser, TV, and queen bed. Sink in the corner. Sink deeply into the mattress. Everything's clean, though, and the folks who run it—the Titus's—seem nice.

Fried catfish, hush puppies and popcorn shrimp at the T & T Family Restaurant, producing a stomachache for me later. Memorial Day Weekend is coming up, and already the river enthusiasts, the ones who could leave home early, are arriving, canoes on top of their cars.

As I drift off to sleep I remember the term for the locals: Arkies. As in the Depression song, "Hey Okie, go tell Arkie, Texas got a job for him out in Californy."

May 24th   Day 38
52.4 miles
Eminence — Johnson's Shut-Ins State Park, Missouri

We eat breakfast downstairs in the dining room of the hotel, which is also a public cafe. Their particular variation on the greasy spoon breakfast is homemade bread and doughnuts, which are okay.

As we ride away into the foggy hills, rolling down the main street,

I see them in an open wooden booth marked TOURIST INFORMATION : bearded men in overalls, smoking cigars. Squinty women in tight jeans and flannel shirts. The locals.

Some copy for a postcard: "We saw the locals, a taciturn lot. Some sit in silence and overalls, smoking cigars and spitting. The men, on the other hand, spend their time drinking and swerving about the narrow roads in pickups or battered old sedans."

Procyon Lotor: the raccoon, masked bandit of the night. Tom the biker had a chipmunk gnaw through his tent while he was asleep and consume or carry away an entire bag of peanuts, one at a time.

Notes on the Missouri Department of Transportation's highway-patching technique: first a heavy oiling, followed by a load of white gravel. Then they wait for traffic to beat it into a road. If it's done right, it's a barely passable road. If it's done sloppily, it's a nightmare to ride on. One of the bikers we met, Jeff, asked a road crew why they did it that way. He was told, "It's cheap." However, we haven't run into many long stretches of bad road. Worst to date was the old highway into Chanute, Kansas.

Some steep hills into Ellington, but it's lovely riding through the dense black oaks, covered with green lichens. At the middle of one hill (like many of them, benched at several points), we stopped so I could adjust Nanci's derailleur. Her rear wheel looks like it badly needs trueing.

In Ellington we enter the semi-fancy Hub, the first eating place on the left, and sit unnoticed among tourists for 15 minutes before leaving and riding further into town. The Ellington Cafe is more what we've been used to, a country dinner of fried chicken with white beans, macaroni and cheese, mashed potatoes, canned corn, and rolls, plus the ubiquitous Dr. Pepper. Nanci had barbecued chicken on a roll for $1; my lunch seemed expensive at $3.20. The chicken was outstanding. All kinds of joshing and local conversation going on. The customary farewell: "Y'all come back, now!" I like that better than Peter's.

Before leaving town we stopped to buy Coleman fuel; I filled our fuel bottle and had to give back half the can to the hardware clerk because we just can't carry more than a pint-and-a-half. On Highway 21 from Ellington, the grades are reasonable, like those out West. Roadcuts, even.

But partway up the first hill, a thunderstorm moves in and very soon we're in the thick of it. A well-placed roadside rest allows us to get under some trees and even read a marker about the genesis of Reynolds County. Nanci falls asleep sitting against the trunk of a pine and I sit in my rain suit and read, dripping on the pages and smearing them with greasy water from my gloves. Eventually the shower slackens, then lets up. We get back out on the nice wide highway and are soon warmed up and dried out. The sun makes a few stabs at us, but dark clouds are still lurking behind the steep ridges all around.

The grades have really calmed down and are acting normal now. We blast through tiny Centerville, noticing a pack of outlaw motorcyclists having a barbecue, and soon turn off the main road on another county road, which gives us a few steep ones before dropping us into Johnson's Shut-Ins State Park. Although they're full, the friendly rangers do make provision for bicyclists in the Organized Youth Camp by the Black River, a large grassy area which we have to ourselves.

We bought a bundle of oak from the park for $1.50 and had a campfire. Later some other campers came near us under cover of darkness and cut down a young live cedar, taking its branches for fuel and leaving the trunk lying in the brush. Report later from their neighbors was that the green wood put out their fire.

Before dark the ranger came by to post a flood warning—he wasn't allowed to tell us not to worry, he said, but it wasn't serious, and he managed to get the message across. Still, we stared thoughtfully at the Black River twenty yards from our tent. We hung our food in a tree, a precaution against *procyon lotors.*

May 25th   Day 39
48 miles
Johnson's Shut-Ins State Park — Bonne Terre, Missouri

Next morning a leisurely reveille, and Krusteaz honey-whole-wheat pancakes for breakfast, then time out for sightseeing. Here is how the shut-ins were formed: A billion years ago, as Carl Sagan would say, the granite plateau of the Ozarks was upthrust, following which it was covered by an ancient sea, which deposited the sediments that became the limestone covering. Over the next hundreds of millions of years streams eroded deep into the limestone, creating the rugged Ozark topography. Only in a few places was the old rock exposed; this is one of them. We saw the light-colored rock, looking very old and wrinkled, constraining the Black River into narrow channels. Then we rode away, trying very hard not to be snobby about our Western rock formations.

These are the St. Francis Mountains. A trail runs from the park all the way to Taum Sauk, Missouri's highest point at 1775 feet. It's part of the Ozark Trail, currently being developed.

Our road followed the Black for a while and was therefore practically flat, compared to the past few days. It started to rain lightly. We passed exposed areas of reddish granite, plus a few houses built from it— reminding me of some of the red stone houses in the Southwest. We rode through tiny Graniteville, then Pilot Knob, where we lunched at an all-you-can-eat place called the Iron Kettle. The owner was very congenial, coming over briefly to sit with us. Good fried chicken and vegetable salads, and it got very busy right after we sat down, due to the after-church crowd.

The mountain of the same name looms over the small roadside town of Pilot Knob, a big square rusty iron ore mill at its base. The peak is just some rocks at the crest of a wooded ridge. The rain grew a little heavier on the way into Farmington, but it was the same nice topography. Kids were walking along the road with buckets and fishing poles.

Farmington is a big town, and we entered it through some beautiful tree-shaded residential streets, lined with old homes. We barely paused in town, but continued on a small country-suburban road to the north. We have now left the TransAmerica Trail and picked up the Great River Central Route. There's no traffic.

Tonight we're sitting in the Bonneville Motel in Bonne Terre, a medium-sized small town whose claim to fame is nearby lead mines. We rode here in a steady drizzle, but now it's raining harder outside, and various items of apparel are hung in the room to dry. Our bikes are leaned against the wall with care, sporting newly-cleaned derailleurs and chains. There's a Miles Davis birthday celebration on the radio, which finally picks up a decent station, KWMU in St. Louis. It's round about midnight.

May 26th   Day 40
60.5 miles
Bonne Terre — Sullivan, Missouri

So far this morning it's not been raining, but it looks like it will any minute. An awful breakfast at Bonneville Restaurant, then a steep climb through the streets of Bonne Terre and what we hope are the last of the Ozarks.

Founded in 1864, Bonne Terre is in a formerly important lead-mining district. A tailings pile, like a huge sand dune, dominates the town's skyline. The mine pits are filled with water, and people scuba-dive in them. Nearby there's a mining museum, which we didn't check out.

As we follow a semi-suburban road the short, steep hills persist. This is Memorial Day, but so far things are fairly quiet. A few pickups go by hauling barbecue grills, and there are smells of grilling meat wafting from certain yards. We still expect it to rain any moment. The road takes some swings along the side of a ridge, affording a great view of the wooded ridges all about.

Again there have been some changes since the route was mapped in 1980—the road up out of Big River from Washington State Park is now unpaved along several considerable sections as far as Route 21. Our 1-1/8″ tires do all right in the gravel, though both of us end up walking for a few hundred yards. The sun is now shining and it's pretty hot and humid. I flick a tick off my leg at our lunch on the front porch of a tiny wooden grocery store in the imperceptible town of Richwoods.

We end up making a steep climb onto a ridge, where we find black oaks and pines like in the deep Ozarks. Holiday traffic—young folks with bare chests and Budweisers, rubber rafts on car tops—thickens as we drop into the Meremac River and proceed to Sullivan, where we camp at a KOA next to the noisy freeway. Kind of expensive: $11, even with our 10% discount. Bartok's *Concerto for Orchestra* plays on KWMU.

Here in Sullivan we had a chance to examine the question of Jesse James's escape: history says that shortly after breakfast on April 3, 1882, James and his cousins Charlie and Robert Ford retired to a parlor in James's St. Joseph, Missouri home. Robert shot Jesse in the back while the outlaw stood on a chair, straightening a crooked picture. Or did he? Some believe it was a hoax, and that James died at the age of 103 in 1951.

Nevertheless everyone agrees that in his prime James used Meremac Caverns as a hideout for his gang between operations. He'd learned about the labyrinthine limestone cave system while a member of Quantrill's Irregulars, a feared guerilla band who staged raids on pro-Union towns during the Civil War.

May 27th Day 41
78.3 miles
Sullivan — Wright City, Missouri

Some clouds this next day but the sun eventually shines as we head north and slightly west toward the Missouri River, hoping all the way that the short but steep hills will go away. At one point in the morning we get lost—or, as Daniel Boone would put it, "bewildered." We're supposed to turn right after crossing the Bourbeuse River, but we end up a mile later in Beaufort ("BOO-furt," a resident corrects my French-fried pronunciation). Going back, we find that the names of the streets have changed a little since the route was mapped. But we make our way through somehow, and descend into Washington on a rather busy road.

Washington looks like an old industrial river town. We settle for more fast food at a Hardee's and then stop by a five-and-dime for some supplies. As I waited to turn into the shopping plaza, I looked into a dingy brick house through taped-up windows, and saw a sad-eyed old woman in the dark, peering out as if she could see through the shining new stores to the ancient Missouri River beyond.

Crossing the Missouri River was awesome, even after all the big rivers we've crossed. This one seemed *immense.* Upstream, on the south bank, there was a white church spire sticking up out of the woods. Downstream, in the sun, the brown river just gleamed.

The biggest mistake of the day was not to wait for lunch until Augusta. Augusta Bottom Road was the first level road we'd been on for awhile, past cornfields with the river bluffs on our left. Up a steep hill, and suddenly two wineries loom, Mantrelle and Mt. Pleasant. We stopped at the latter, founded in the 1850s, and tasted two wines, Seyval Blanc and Steuben; they were like a Sauvignon Blanc and a White Zinfandel, respectively. Also there's a cheese and sausage shop right behind the old brick winery building. "Historic" Augusta, founded in 1855, is a cute little town full of antique shops, bread stands, and even a gourmet coffee shop. The woman at Mt. Pleasant told us this is the oldest wine-producing region in the United States.

Riding on through the wooded countryside, while we were climbing what proved to be the last steep hill of the day, a fellow in a pickup turning into his driveway stopped and waved us down. His friendly, slightly buck-toothed smile, shaded by a drooping brown moustache, looked familiar to me. He said he was a laborer at a construction site, but that he owned 40 acres, and one of his three kids was a high school bicycle racer. He invited us to dinner and to camp in his yard, and seemed a little disappointed when we told him we had to get to Troy. "What are you in such a hurry for?" he asked. It made me think—why? We have to get home on July 9th, that's why.

Toward Wright City, at I-70, the road once again got busier, and also flatter, with more cornfields stretching in both directions. We checked into an inexpensive, clean but small motel room in Wright. Riding across the freeway we saw our first blacks in a while, in an interracial clump of hoodlum types loitering around some motorcycles and battered sedans. St. Louis is about 40 miles east of here—the urban influence must penetrate deeper into the countryside along the interstates.

Over dinner we learned that this place is on the old Boone's Lick Trail, blazed by Daniel when Kentucky got too crowded for him in the early 19th century. Pauldingsville, four miles south, was once the first stage stop west of the Missouri River. That's why, a century later in 1924, Bob "Big Boy" Cheyney started his Big Boy Restaurant. It's a nationwide franchise now, but this claims to be the original, unaffiliated with any of the others. A big wooden dining room, with plenty of big tables, gives it an agreeable lumber-camp mess hall look. So do the friendly waitresses and an all-you-can-eat family dinner and breakfast, served buffet-style on an enclosed patio. And *real* butter and *real* half-and-half, home-baked muffins and cornbread.

Back when we crossed the Kansas-Missouri line, I felt somehow that the overwhelming friendliness we'd encountered on the plains and in the Flint Hills would suddenly come to a halt. It didn't, really, although we noticed an increasing indifference on the part of the drivers as we came closer to St. Louis, and more disaffected youth driving in a surly manner, clashing gears or "patching out" or just throttling up as they passed, to unnerve us. Instances of outright friendliness became more intense yet more isolated, and as we entered Wright City, I had the first instance of outright hostility: an oncoming compact pickup driver gave me a middle finger as he passed, for no apparent reason. Mostly it's just impatience or silly drunken exuberance, like the girls who whooped at us from their car windows, or the guy who had to wait as I passed a fishing pull-out on the Bourbeuse River, yelling "Come on, move it." Share the road with someone slower, buddy. The river's not going anywhere.

May 28th   Day 42
49.3 miles
Wright City — Clarksville, Missouri

We called home and talked to Barb, who's sitting house for us. The cherry trees in the yard are blooming, and the dog's all right.

Pay phones are still a dime around here, in line with the rest of Missouri's generally low price structure. This morning it's raining possums and turtles outside as we finish our Big Boy breakfast buffet. We get the bikes packed and then stall for time in our room, watching Billy Joel on MTV, until the rain turns to a light drizzle. By 10 a.m. we're proceeding north again—it's in the low 60s but climbing fast and combined with the final ups and downs of Missouri's hill country we heat up right away. Gradually the rain ceases and there's a hint of blue.

In 12 miles we're at Troy, Missouri, on the Cuivre (Copper) River. A former encampment of the Sac and Fox Indians, the site was fortified by early settlers in response to British-backed Indian attacks during the War of 1812. The Indians were ready allies of any opponents of the Americans, being a bit chagrined at their cession of land rights to the settlers from Kentucky. They wanted it all back. Today Troy is a legal and commercial center for the surrounding farms and cattle ranches. We stopped for a few minutes at a historical site, an old log cabin in the lawn-like town square, then went to a convenience store to make some phone calls in hopes of arranging a bed-and-breakfast situation in Hannibal.

Cresting a hill north of Troy, we were treated to a view of low dome-like hills arranged in a row across the rolling landscape. The wooded summits of each looked almost trimmed, giving the tops a hedge-like appearance.

Carcasses of possum and skunk grotesquely splayed on the edge of the road; also, mashed turtles, and some live ones, lumbering across the road, that we didn't hold much hope for. Like us, they may be heading for the Mississippi River, which isn't far off now.

Small cornfields on the lower slopes and bottomlands. Well-to-do homes with sometimes vast, neatly-manicured lawns. I had thought that lawn-mowing, which we've seen a lot of in Missouri, was something of a fetish. All those weekend warriors astride their tractor mowers. But, we're informed, it's really necessary to keep down the populations of chiggers and ticks.

The small towns of Brussels and New Hope offer no services. Finally in Paynesville there's a spiffy public phone building on the corner. I make arrangements for brother Dick to send his camera to us in Hannibal, and also for us to stay in the Fifth Street Bed & Breakfast there Thursday and Friday nights.

In Paynesville we meet George Norvall, a big overweight guy with a Mountain Dew bottle sticking out of the side pocket of his overalls, who drives a gravel truck for Pike County, and has seen loaded cyclists on this road before. He suggests that, rather than turn here and go through Eulia to the town of Louisiana on county roads H & D, we stay on W for eight miles to Clarksville, and ride up the river on 79. His reasons were as follows: Route 79 used to have a lot more traffic on it before several more bridges were constructed downstream. Also, parts of D were being paved and there was a great deal of dumptruck traffic on it—a windy, hilly road which he said was ten times more dangerous than 79. And there's Clarksville, a historic town. To which we added, we'd had enough of the rolling wooded hill country and are ready for the Mississippi, even if it means climbing some bluffs. We took his advice, and about a mile down W there he was again, pulled off the road in his red dumptruck, with more information about which campsites to look for and which ones to avoid.

We rode what seemed a very short way to Clarksville, catching a glimpse from on high of the silver thread of the river before rolling downhill into the town. We went across the tracks to the riverside and gazed, full of wonder, at the Father of Waters.

A few blocks north along the river a kindly Shell attendant directed us to Lock & Dam 24, after piling local promotional literature into our hands. We sat for what must have been two hours, watching an upbound towboat and its 15 barges negotiate the lock. The Army Corps of Engineers has provided a sheltered platform with spotter scopes where you can sit and watch the action.

We made friends with Jim, a towboat deckhand waiting to reboard the *Jane Huffman*. Thirty-four-year-old Jim, who said he differed from the usual illiterate deckhand from Arkansas or Mississippi by having two years of college under his hatband, told us the following facts: each barge measures 35 x 195 feet and weighs about 400 tons empty. 1500 tons of coal, or 20,000 bushels of grain, or similar amounts of other commodities, fill each barge. There are about 27 locks along the stretch between St. Paul, Minnesota and St. Louis, Missouri, below which the river gets wider and deeper so dams aren't necessary to control flooding. It takes about 15 days for a round trip between these two ports. Each "tow," or towboat and its barges, takes about an hour to complete each "lockage," or locking process. The towboats range from 3000-9000 hp., and below St. Louis, tows often reach 40 or 50 barges, pushed rather than pulled to avoid whipping in the cross-currents and winds.

There is only a five-foot clearance in the lock's width, and since the towboat (never call it a tug!) and its 15 barges (three abreast by five long) are 1200 feet long, and the locks on the Mississippi are just under 800 feet long, the boat can push only 12 of its barges into the lock at one time. Deckhands then unhook them, the towboat backs out, the lock closes, fills (for upbound traffic—lowers for downbound), opens at the other end, and a winch on the lock pulls the barges through. Only then can the boat and the rest of the barges go through. The boat pushes the barges hard up against the 12 in front, engines churning, and deckhands rewire them together. Then they move on, and the next towboat in line (often there's three or four waiting, and more coming around the bends up or down river) moves in for locking. Each boat carries two pilots, an engineer, a cook, and six deckhands, who work six hours on, six hours off. The pilot makes $200/day, and deckhands up to $100. They often work 30 days on, 15 off.

Jim kept saying, "The railroads really hate this," pointing to the barges, loaded with piles of shiny black stoker coal, headed for St. Paul. On the return trip they'll carry grain. The coal came down the Ohio River from Kentucky or Pennsylvania. Barges also carry scrap metal, fertilizer, petroleum products, gravel, aluminum, sugar, salt, molasses, even liquid methane.

Jim went back to the bar for "my last beer for 45 days," and we sat watching, feeling very much in the heart of a vast, ancient commercial network. Indians had used the river, of course, and 18th-century French trappers in their *pirogues*. Steam-powered riverboats were on the water by 1811, plying the Ohio and Mississippi rivers only four years after Robert Fulton floated the first powered vessel in the Hudson at Clairmont. The river of that day was treacherous, with plenty of hidden snags and sandbars. Even though the riverboat was designed to float *on* the water and not *in* it, the average life of a 19th-century boat was 18 months. If they didn't rip a hole in the wooden hull, their temperamental boilers, burning 30-40 cords/day, would often blow up.

But the river trade caused the river towns' populations to swell, as timber, iron ore and cotton moved quickly and cheaply 7 m.p.h. upstream and 10-12 m.p.h. down, not much slower than today. But modern towboats can carry a lot more cargo, can run for two weeks on their 100,000 gallons of diesel fuel, and are presumably safer to operate.

This river system extends from New Orleans to St. Paul, almost 2500 miles on the Mississippi alone. Then there's the Ohio River to Pittsburgh, the Illinois River to Chicago, the Missouri to Sioux City, Iowa (US's second longest) and other rivers to Tulsa and elsewhere.

Jim's back, definitely boozed. He shows us a picture of his daughter, four-year-old Becky, and talks to me about his aspirations to become a writer. I encourage him to start keeping a journal. He tells us many stories, like when they were tied to a tree on the banks of the Missouri, where you can't navigate at night. In his words, the crew was relaxing, "getting high," when a runaway or loose barge piled into them, causing mass confusion. He claims it's real easy to get maimed or killed out there, showing us a smashed finger and listing ruptures and rib fractures he's had. But, he intends to go on from this to sea with the Merchant Marine. He warns us about the dangers of the road, leaning over to me confidentially and saying, "You got a real beautiful wife there, you dig?" We exchange addresses and part company.

> Gonna pick up a few of these empties
> Just as soon as we know where they lay—
> Towboat picking up barges
> On a long hot summer day.
>
> For every day I work on the Illinois River
> Get a half-day off with pay—
> Towboat picking up barges
> On a long hot summer day.
> —John Hartford

Since there's dark clouds blowing up fast from the south, we cancel plans to ride upriver to a campground and check into the Duvall Best Western Motel right there by Lock 24 and across the street from the Skyride, an old ski lift up to the highest point on the river, 600 feet above the water on the surrounding wooded bluffs. Mediocre dinner at the adjoining Duvall Restaurant, then back to our room to watch a great lightning display and listen to the towboats hooting in the dark, the barges booming as they strike the sides of the lock. On the radio from

St. Louis the Kronos Quartet plays a string arrangement of Jimi Hendrix's "Purple Haze."

It's pouring rain, the river's high, and the dam gates are wide open. The water in our room runs brown, and tastes terrible.

Chapter Five:
The River Rats

May 29th   Day 43
48.6 miles
Clarksville — Hannibal, Missouri

It felt good to be finally riding along the Mississippi, just like in my California fantasies. The campground a few miles north where we had been thinking of staying looked flooded, pools of water standing among the trees. It's a good road with excellent visibility. We climb bluffs, and descend them, mostly paralleling the railroad at a greater or lesser distance. In about ten miles our route converges with the road we would have taken from Eulia, had we followed the Great River Bike Map instead of George Norvall's detour along the Great River Road. The junction is by a chemical plant, which we learn is the largest operating nitric acid factory in the world. From one of the many smokestacks, thick brown gas emerges. The smell I had noticed, and thought maybe to be decaying vegetation—somewhat like chamomile—is perhaps a by-product of this industry. Some big trucks wheel about.

After another mile we're riding between the limestone bluffs, thickly wooded along the crest, and the railroad tracks which are right on the river. It looks as if the river has no more room to rise—another foot and it would be over rails and road. A train roars by, northbound, and we've completed the 12 miles to Louisiana. This is another old industrial town, and another Hardee's for breakfast, several miles west of town. There we met again the nice fat family we'd seen talking with Jim at the Clarksville Lock. They're on their way to Hannibal, too.

After Louisiana we climb over a bluff, then we're jogging inland to cross the Salt River, and there are several very steep bluff climbs. It's hot and humid, and we're both sweating freely.

Then a run along the river, one final bluff climb, past the "Mark Twain Caverns," and down the hill into Hannibal. It's not hard to find the Fifth Street Bed & Breakfast, an Italianate Victorian home built during 1858-1866 by John Garth, a friend of Mark Twain's (naturally) on a tree-shaded side street. The bikes go in the parlor, which is kind of unruly, one wall piled with empty cartons. Host Lance Zedric is dressed in a tank top and gym shorts, a muscular red-haired guy who comes on like a friendly fraternity brother. He shows me the room, and then we talk about teaching English until I remember that Nanci waits on the sidewalk with the packs, forgotten.

Later, while Nanci walks downtown to the historic area, I ride her bicycle west out Market Street to Mike's Lock and Key, the only bike shop in town. Past some old mobile homes, some vacant old buildings, and other junk for a few miles, then Mike's—a cluttered little shop with bikes hanging from the ceiling, some parts piled about, and Randy the bike mechanic, a short-haired swarthy fellow with tattoos. I wonder how much he knows about bikes. I go into the back of the shop to select some new rear tires, since ours are cut up pretty badly. I buy 1-1/4"s, since they don't have any 1-1/8"s, a tube, and some oil. When I'm back out on the floor, and Nanci's bike is behind the counter already, I lean back to point something out and the owner, Mike, hobbling on a cane, prevents me from going back. He points to the sign that says "Authorized Personnel Only."

After the walk back to Fifth Street I need another shower. It's pretty humid here. On her return, Nanci complains of being whistled at from passing cars.

We ate lunch at a restaurant in a big Gothic building, the Missouri Territory, where we had a "California Croissant" from an indifferent waitress in a huge dining room, empty save for us. Pink napkins and tablecloths.

There are a lot of derelicts around Hannibal—river rats, they're called. Here's a woman pushing a baby, yelling at a man in an undershirt who's following her and drinking from a quart of beer. Pinched, wasted faces.

Deciding to have our bottle of Augusta wine with cheese on the Fifth Street porch, we walk through town looking to buy some crackers. Finally we have to settle on Ritz crackers from a cramped liquor store that smells like cigarettes and B.O. Nice time on the porch, though, drinking the wine and chatting in the tropical dusk.

May 30th   Day 44
A Day Off In Hannibal

Next morning Lance serves us breakfast, a rather disappointing affair of weak coffee, doughnuts, and hard-boiled eggs. Then we walk downtown and tour the Mark Twain Home and Museum. Twain, it goes without saying, spent most of his young years here. It is reported that one night late in his life, in India, he said, "All that goes to make the me in me is a small Missouri village on the other side of the globe." He also said:

> Travel is fatal to prejudice, bigotry and narrow-mindedness
> ...and many of our people need it sorely on these accounts.
> Broad, wholesome, charitable views of men and things
> cannot be acquired by vegetating in one little corner of the
> earth all one's lifetime.

And:

> I thought the matter over and concluded I could do it [learn
> to ride an old high-wheel bicycle]. So I went down and
> bought a barrel of Pond's Extract and a bicycle. Even when
> I could not hit a wagon, I could hit a dog that came to see
> me practice. They all liked to see me practice, and they all
> came, for there was very little going on in our neighborhood
> to entertain a dog.

> Get a bicycle. You will not regret it if you live.

> —this last from "Taming the Bicycle"

Hannibal was founded in 1819, on land ceded by the British, who got it from the French, whose traders had been traipsing around and trapping for fur since the late 17th century. Some of the original land parcels were given by the government to farmers who had lost their land to the 1811 earthquake in New Madrid, Missouri. In 1835 a man named William Muldrow planned a town called Marion City, eight miles north of Hannibal, and sold lots to Easterners who arrived in 1836 to find their land under water. Many of them then settled in Hannibal. Shortly before Twain's birth in 1835, the John Clemens family moved to Missouri. ("The state was new," wrote Sam, "and needed attractions.") They moved to Hannibal in 1839.

To those familiar with the Philadelphia area, I can describe our day off in Hannibal like a vacation in a slightly more spacious version of a working-class neighborhood such as Manayunk or Fishtown. Narrow streets, battered old sedans cruising at Mach 2, laying rubber at every opportunity, rock music blasting from car windows, motorcycles, and faded, warping, peeling, vacant wooden houses with weeds in the ascendance everywhere. Missouri, by the way, is one of the few states that hasn't gained population since World War II.

The town's historic district features some restored mid-19th century buildings, and establishments mostly named along the imaginative lines of the Mark Twain Dinette featuring Mark Twain Fried Chicken, Tom Sawyer's Car Wash, and Aunt Polly's Miniature Golf. On the whole the surroundings are very shabby, with lots of liquor stores and bars. Park benches stood amidst islands of litter on the green.

The town suffers from a confusion of literary and physical reality: there are signs everywhere commemorating the location of various incidents from *Tom Sawyer* and *Huckleberry Finn*. One historic plaque by the river, erected in 1934, points out the place where Huck Finn and (BLANK) Joe set out on their raft trip. The word chiseled out and painted over is obviously "nigger."

In a small bookshop we bought paperback copies of *Life on the Mississippi* and *Huckleberry Finn*.

Later in the day we raced down to the dock to catch a riverboat, only to hear its whistle and see it backing out into the river, three blocks away. So I went back to Fifth Street and worked on my bike instead, changing tire and tube and chain, while Nanci went shopping for souvenirs. We went out to the bike shop to pick up Nanci's bike, signed Mike's logbook, then proceeded west on busy, potholed Market Street to the AAA on legendary Highway 61. Brother Dick's camera was waiting there, but AAA policies had changed with longitude and they were unable to trade us American Express traveler's checks for a personal check. We rode downtown to several banks but they would barely speak to us, let alone succor a pair of credit-rich, cash-poor Californians.

So we returned to the riverboat *Mark Twain* for a dinner cruise on the Mississippi. Cocktails on the upper deck, then a roast beef buffet below. The speed with which they broke down the steam tables was amazing (no second helpings, that's for sure). An ersatz Dixieland trio—piano, trombone, and drums—entertained with old pop tunes. A fat orange sun slowly dropped behind the bluffs to the west as we cruised around a heavily-wooded, flooded island and came about under the big steel bridge that crosses from Hannibal to Illinois, thinking about life on the Mississippi.

May 31st   Day 45
70.6 miles
Hannibal, Missouri — Nauvoo, Illinois

Next morning another well-intentioned breakfast from Lance—it turns out that he's only been operating the bed & breakfast for a month, taking over a previously-successful operation with his silent partner Tom. They'll need a lot more style and grace if they plan to make a name for themselves with the finicky set that usually patronizes this type of establishment. Our beds weren't made up, there were no fresh towels; on the other hand it is homey and relaxed—Lance offered us the washer/dryer, which was a real blessing—but the service was, well, very low-profile. The rooms were clean, but the porch and grounds were just beginning to show the edges of neglect. Lance seems to have his hands full. Nice books around, including a 19th-century copy of Caesar's *Gallic Commentaries* by the downstairs color TV. It cost us $40/night—a bargain by California standards.

We rode through town and over the bridge into Illinois. As we stopped to check the map, a couple in a big car pulling out of the Colonial Motel directed us along the river rather than loop out into the farm country where our bike route directed us. It was a good road, the Great River Road, designated the Lincoln Heritage Trail. We rode just a few miles of freeway then cut off on a mostly level road north into Quincy. We rode past big soybean companies, filling the air with the sweet steamy smell of cooking beans. We also rode through blasts of cool air from underground warehouses excavated into the bluffs. Quincy is a big industrial town on the river, with some good architecture and building by German immigrant craftsmen—plenty of stonework and woodcarving. From our route, the Holiday Inn looked like the best bet for breakfast, so I went in to ask if we could pull our bikes into the entryway. The desk clerks let us park them in the executive offices, leaning up against a richly-panelled wall.

Riding out of town north along the river we found the road closed due to flooding, picnic tables and telephone booths awash, so we diverted up the bluff, through thick greenery, and rolled along the highway above till we rejoined our mapped route. Young corn was growing everywhere. These little towns look like they have something left: neatly-kept older homes, many with turrets, cupolas, and even stained glass. Some have kitchens detached at the rear of the homes, Southern-style. Big shade trees. On Sunday mornings, folks in cool white dresses and gray suits cluster outside the wooden or brick churches.

From Warsaw north the river is more park-like, with frequent rest stops and no industry. We saw water falling down limestone ledges on its way to join the river. Some bicyclists were rolling down river, and a few water skiers were even out.

Entering Nauvoo there were billboards promoting the town's historic attractions, and Visitor Centers for both the Church of Jesus Christ of Latter Day Saints and the *Reorganized* Church of JC-LDS. Then came the State Park, several hundred acres of flats, with the bluffs rising to the east out of the woods. We rode up a hill, curving to the right, and came into Nauvoo, glimpsing behind and below us a big eastward bend in the Mississippi. Craving showers, we immediately checked into the Hotel Nauvoo, built as a residence in 1840 and recently restored. It was dominated this Saturday night by a big bicycle outing, comprised of club members from several Illinois towns. Nanci went to buy bread and cheese for tomorrow's lunch, then we went to the hotel's big dining hall for a huge all-we-could-eat buffet. Plenty of fresh vegetables.

Later we walked around the small town, watching the sun set over the river. We spoke with a young boy and his dog in the park, then walked to the site of Nauvoo Temple. There was a miniature reconstruction of the Mormon Temple, and the archaeologically excavated remains of the original foundation. It was built during the years 1841-46, when the Mormons, or "Saints" as they prefer to be called, paused in Nauvoo on their way west, swelling the population to 15,000. The temple was 128' x 88' and 60' high, built by volunteer labor and craftsmen paid with trade goods.

But the Saints were run out of town upon its completion. An "unidentified incendiary" fired the temple on October 9, 1848, leaving only the stone walls. (In town there is a home with a plaque proclaiming it to have belonged to Joseph Agnew, "suspected temple arsonist.") In 1849 a group of French economic communitarians, the Icarian Society, used the partially reconstructed temple ruins as their headquarters until a tornado blew it down in May 1850.

Two young men in white shirts and ties sat on a bench nearby. One came over, identified by his black plastic badge as Elder Leyva, and gave us a brochure on the temple and another on Mormon beliefs. He seemed vague on details, but told us that the Reorganized JC-LDS are the ones who stayed in 1846. What did they have to do to stay? He didn't know. We had been told by Lance we'd be Joseph Smith'd to death here, but we heard hardly anything about the founder of the Mormon Church.

One store in Nauvoo sold "Genealogy Supplies," used by the Saints when tracing their ancestors for posthumous baptism.

June 1st   Day 46
79.4 miles
Nauvoo — Galesburg, Illinois

Leaving Nauvoo it was already 75 degrees at 8 a.m. We decided to deviate slightly from the Bikecentennial route by staying on the Great River Road, closer to the Mississippi. We passed through little towns like Dallas City and Lomax, where everyone seemed to be at church. Not much traffic. Getting back on the marked route, we followed our map onto some little farm road, only to find the pavement ending a few miles in. We threaded our way out through the right-angle turns, and got back on route. Passed by a large installation of prefab metal warehouse-sized sheds, looking very new. Earth still being moved to put in more—same rows of doors, bare earth about, some machinery here and there, quite a big operation for these parts. Hog barns? Didn't really smell like it yet.

Riding into Oquawka, on the Mississippi, Nanci stopped to buy some strawberries from a guy sitting on his lawn, then we went to a Tastee Delight for some hamburgers, fries, and ice cream. When I went inside to pick up our order, a table of good old boys (and one good young boy in training) started asking about our bike trip. One guy asked, "Who's sponsorin' ya?" I said, "Nobody—we are." So he asked me for a business card, which I gave him, then he slapped a $20 bill on the formica table, which he wouldn't let me refuse. "Now I'm sponsoring you," he said.

Henry Harris, of Harris Construction and Siding Company in Oquawka, Illinois. Free Estimates. All he wanted, he said, was a phone call at the end. I took his picture outside, next to his truck with its plastic logo on the door. Skinny, toothless Henry, last seen drinking coffee at the Tastee Delight in Oquawka.

"You ridin' through these ol' river rat towns?" asked Henry's young, husky red-haired helper (who used to live in Barstow, California). "Better watch out for Keithsburg."

We talked with a couple and their teenage son, who are out bicycling for the day from their home in Viola. He works in the Quad Cities (Davenport, Moline, Bettendorf, Rock Island) and she teaches school in a nearby small town. They told us that their winter gets down to zero every night, the Mississippi freezes solid, and they ice-fish on it. Snow on the ground all season, and they cross-country ski on the cold, granular stuff. They assured us that Highway 34 was a good one for bicycling; we've decided to cut east here to Galesburg, the biggest town around, and ask my dad to wire us cold cash for our resupply of traveler's checks. Unlike the AAA and the Hannibal financial institutions, he'll take our personal check.

The road turns out to be good as far as Monmouth but US 34 is pretty busy, with no shoulder. However, a tailwind pushes our speed to 15-20 mph, and the entire 30 miles is over quickly. We get a sliver of a shoulder close to Galesburg, and most of the traffic is outbound, on the other side of the road; they've had their Railroad Days celebration that weekend, and lines of antique cars and motorcycles are heading west.

In Galesburg we pig out on Wendy's potatoes and salad bar, and decide on the Holiday Inn for convenience. Reading billboards pays, I learned: I saw their rate advertised as $39.95, and when the clerk charged me $46, I mentioned the advertised rate. "Oh, all you have to do is mention it," she said. That night we watched *Gremlins* on HBO, starring Hoyt Axton, and *Fame*, as the wind shifted from east to north and blew all the hot, humid air south.

Chapter Six:
Tightening the Farm Belt; or,
Why the East is Green

June 2nd   Day 47
46.8 miles
Galesburg — Kewanee, Illinois

Next day was sunny, breezy and cool—perfect for riding (well, maybe perfect without the breeze). But we had to wait for the wireload of money to travel from the Mellon Bank in Haverford, Pennsylvania, to the First Galesburg National Bank and Trust. Everyone was pleasantly patient, and the money came in about 12:30 p.m. Meanwhile Nanci took a jacuzzi in the Holidome, and I stayed in the room mechanicking. I shortened our chains by another two links—it seems they shift better, and the chain is quieter, when there's a bit of spring tension when the chain's on the smallest sprockets. There was enough tension that Nanci had to assist me by holding the jockey wheel forward a bit each time I closed the chain. Another good reason for not travelling alone.

Galesburg is the home of Carl Sandburg, and while we were waiting in front of the bank a woman who worked for the local paper came up and told us we should visit his memorial. "Galesburg's a railroad town," she told us, apropos of nothing.

We picked up our traveler's checks and rode out of town on some farm roads. Since we were off route, we decided to aim straight for the Illinois River, cross it, camp, and next day hit the Bikecentennial route where it headed south on the other side. But the headwind kept our speed down to 10 mph, and we soon realized we wouldn't make the river before dark. So we cut north toward Kewanee, and by early evening were riding through Bishop Hill.

Founded in 1846, Bishop Hill was an experiment in communal living led by Swedish religious dissident Eric Janson. Their farm prospered, but Janson was shot in 1850, some say because of an increasingly dissolute lifestyle, and the settlement dissolved. It's been restored into a state historic site now, with some beautiful old homes and public buildings like the Old Colony Church, with walnut pews and 100 primitive paintings by Olaf Krans. There's a nice statue of Janson in the park. The brick buildings, some with faded advertisements painted on their sides, shone a fiery red in the low sun.

We saw some private residences, and asked the bartender, tending the only thing open at 7 p.m. on Monday evening, if there was a bed and breakfast around. He said that someone was getting one going, but it wasn't open yet. So we headed back into the wind, slanting golden sunbeams at our back, for the 12 miles of rolling fields to Kewanee, "Hog Capital of the Nation."

Johnson Sauk Trail State Park is seven miles north of Kewanee and it was a perfect night for camping, but darkness had caught us, so we checked in at a brand-new, expensive ($41) motor lodge. Pigged out (like Kewanee hogs) at the local Dairy Queen, 99 cents for burger and fries, then I crashed while Nanci watched a Steve Martin movie on Cinemax, *All of Me.*

June 3rd Day 48
87.8 miles
Kewanee — Cornell, Illinois

Another perfect morning, but we slept in till 7:30. Breakfast next door, then more farm roads and low rolling hills 40 miles to the Illinois River at Henry. Lunch in the park, with fresh cherries and lemonade.

Some of our constant companions on the road—familiar sights by now—are the corrugated, galvanized Butler bins, and the more expensive-looking A.O. Smith HarvestStore system silos with their enameled porcelain look, like a huge vase. Comes with color-coordinated accessories, no doubt, like the attachments to a catalog store drill. Then there are the long white fertilizer tanks full of anhydrous ammonia, and other assorted reapers, cultivators, plows, seed drills, grain conveyors, and tractors. We're also used to the slow gazes of cattle, heads rotating to follow us, the squealing panic of pigs, the quick scurry of prairie dog or cottontail rabbit, and the invisible rustle of snake, lizard, or who knows what in the roadside grass.

Then there's the people's stares—like someone wrote, you really become part of the scenery when you tour on a bike. And some farmers, who aren't used to treating the land as scenery, can't figure what to make of us. We get everything from excited honks (sometimes unnerving) to kids' waves, to blank stares, but the farmers generally confine themselves to casual waves or indifference. Turning on one road, we saw it totally taken up by a giant combine, headed our way. He pulled over into the grass, though, and waved.

I've always figured that friendliness to us results from familiarity with our kind, but on second thought we are on a well-mapped and relatively well-traveled bicycle route. With a few minor exceptions, through everywhere we've ridden so far go probably several hundred other two-wheeled tourists every year. Maybe the locals are just bored with bicyclists. Anyway, they aren't rushing out to greet us, invite us into dinner, and write us up in their small-town newspapers.

Although the old peaked-roof frame houses next to the fields appear to belong to the farmers, I think that they lease much of the croplands from third parties—banks, or in-town professionals. The roads are generally good through here.

This is an incredibly rich stretch of arable land, but it seems that all the corn and soybeans are grown as cattle and hog feed.

School's out, and these kids are trying to figure out what to do. Jetting around on their BMX's, perhaps condemned to attend vacation Bible School a few days a week, or playing semi-pro little league.

So many cemeteries—we are in Spoon River country, and I'm reminded of Edgar Lee Masters's eponymous *Anthology:* all the epitaphs, the testimonials by the deceased, revealing the little parts they played in the web of life.

> Life all around me here in the village:
> Tragedy, constancy, heroism, failure—
> All in the loom, and oh what patterns!
> Woodlands, meadows, streams and rivers—
> Blind to all of it all my life long.
> —from "Petit, the Poet" (1915)

At last we're camping again. Even with the extra work, it's a welcome change from those boxy drywall motels. The weather this afternoon was diamond-perfect, crystal clear. A little warmer than yesterday. We are finely tuned to weather information and rumors from all sources, and there is talk of a few thundershowers—"thundery" weather as the woman on the TV weather channel called it—tonight and the next few days, but with the cooler and generally fair weather persisting at least through the weekend. Who knows? We're always wondering, but for now it's okay. So we're riding along, side by side, singing to pass the time along these quiet roads: "The Weight," and all the old Beatles songs we can remember.

Crossing the Illinois River at Henry, we climbed the low river bluffs back onto the prairie, which is a little less rolling than before. No more cattle or pigs—this is all corn and beans. "Some of the richest farmland in the world," says the narrative on our map.

In Wenona we pause to refresh, and two young girls seem surprised that I know the name of their "little town," being all the way from

California. I just looked at the map, girls, honest. Old-time grocery store with 25-cent Cokes.

Young guy and his nine-month pregnant wife, kids in tow, stop to talk. "Where youse from?" he asks, revealing his Chicago origins. His wife's parents live right out west of town, on the farm road we rode in on. They say they ride bicycles too, towing the two kids in a trailer.

Later we're at the Bayou Bluff campground outside of Cornell. A very well-equipped facility on the Vermillion River—showers, tennis courts, a rec room with ping pong and piano, fishing, and more. It costs us $9, and instead of hanging our food, we're invited by the woman manager to stash it in a vacant camper.

Exactly five weeks from tomorrow, we'll be home. 1500 miles remain.

June 4th   Day 49
88 miles
Cornell, Illinois — Kentland, Indiana

Cloudy morning, with the usual east wind. There's nothing in Cornell, so we ride 15 miles to Odell for breakfast. Friendly place, with some small-town jokes on the menu, some of which will be reproduced here:

HOW SMALL IS SMALL?

You know you are in a small town when:
— the airport is terraced;
— Third Street is the end of town;
— the editor and the publisher of the newspaper carry a camera at all times;
— you don't use your turn signal because everyone knows where you're going;
— you dial a wrong number and talk for 15 minutes anyway;
— you can't walk for exercise because every car that passes offers you a ride;
— you are run off Main Street by a combine;
— you write a check on the wrong bank and it covers it for you anyway;
— someone asks how you feel and then listens to what you say.

We're 90 miles from Chicago via the interstate we just crossed, and here in the Town Hall Restaurant there are tables of women as well as the usual men's club. This region of the country offers "American fries"—sliced fried potatoes—and cinnamon toast on every breakfast menu.

I really got tired of hearing, "Looks like you're going to get wet." We waited out the first shower at the cafe in Odell; then, as we rode east and south, it began to rain heavily. We made it another ten miles to Campus, where we took temporary shelter beneath the scrawny eaves of the post office. Unlike the cafe in Odell, none of the buildings in this town have any kind of awning or covered area in front, so we press ourselves against the wall, trying to stay out of the drips. All the houses have ceramic deer as lawn decorations, poised in attitudes of alertness.

Lunch at Cullan: our cook and server was a salty old unshaven fellow from South Carolina, with an all-you-can-eat spaghetti special—tasted pretty good to us. After we were about done, his regular waitress showed up—a silent old woman with twisted arthritic fingers.

Just before Ashkum it began to pour. We rode for a while, getting thoroughly drenched, then took shelter in a corn crib by the roadside. It was a well-timed move, for the rain intensified into a blinding wall of water, and the lightning began striking all around us. We were in pretty dry quarters, although our feet and tires were covered with thick sticky mud. A decent trade.

Twenty minutes later we were back on the road, straight through Ashkum and south along the muddy brown Iroquois River for a few miles before crossing it on an old steel-girder bridge. Some affluent homes along its banks, and thicker vegetation. The landscape today has looked remarkably like Kansas in that the trees are scarcer, the horizons barer and flatter, and we can tell upcoming towns by the groves of trees and water tanks in the distance, today nearly lost in the thick white haze.

The land here feels broad and low, and we're riding close to the ground, without the vistas or steep embankments we Westerners are used to. Little yellow-bellied birds fly about, folding their wings to dart like missiles. Nanci can tell when water's nearby by the presence of "walking" birds.

The map tells us that Iroquois is a town with a four-figure population and all services, same as Sheldon three miles south, but Iroquois turns out to have 200 people and minimal services, and Sheldon is the same. A friendly guy pulls up to tell us that our best eastward bet is Kentland, "fifteen miles down the road. You looked like you needed some directions, with your maps unfolded there." It turns out to be nine level miles, three on US 52 and six on US 24. The Illinois stretch of 24 is a divided highway at first with eroded but rideable shoulders. As soon as we crossed into Indiana we passed an old sign: "Hoosier hospitality is no accident," and right away some cows rushed over to greet us. Suddenly there's a wonderfully smooth, wide shoulder like a bike lane. We race into Kentland as it gets duskier, car headlights coming on, and I stop at the first restaurant to ask some local cops where to stay. "Turn left at the light, and there's two of them." Which would you recommend? "The Tri-Way." Why? "You won't like the smell of goat meat at the other one." This potentially ethnic slur doesn't get explained. The Tri-Way, on busy US 61, is nice.

Here in Newton County, they've just closed down the nudist camp. Founded in the 40s as a low-key, health-oriented resort, the new owners renamed it Naked City, opened it to truck drivers and other casual onlookers, and ran Miss Nude America and Miss Nude Teenybopper contests. They were calling it "Club Bare" when it was finally closed.

All these towns have their mottos, and it's no different here: "Kentland—Where Agriculture and Industry Meet." Nothing but corn and soybeans, stretching into infinity. The uncultivated fields show rich black earth, and lots of standing water. What corn's been planted is knee-high. The Hoosier State is safe and predictable.

June 5th   Day 50
61.9 miles
Kentland — Logansport, Indiana

US 24 was so good to us last night that we stayed with it this morning. Although the shoulder wasn't quite as smooth, it was a lot better than some. We had a slight tailwind and really highballed. Plenty of towns along here to duck into in case it rains.

Saw the Wolcott Mansion in the town of the same name, commemorating a 19th-century businessman. Big white paint-peeling Italianate Victorian structure, like Fifth Street in Hannibal. Nanci notices that many of the homes through the farmlands here need a paint job. In Wolcott we pause for juice and sweet rolls, and listen to the eternal farmers talking about planting, cultivating, and how much rain fell where. Lots of their fields are flooded right now. "Still," one immense bearded fellow says, "if it's between too much and not enough rain, I'll take too much." But some haven't been able to plant yet.

While we talk, it's pouring outside—the street is literally turning into a river. We drink tea, write cards, and wait. We learn there's a ribbon factory in town, specializing in bows. Satellite dishes are also made nearby, and wooden game boxes—we even passed the place where they make those ceramic deer. US 24 definitely is showing us a different side of this country—still fields and farm buildings, but lots more industry, and more big highways.

Guy in Wolcott cafe tells us about the local "rabbit scam": con men were setting people up with breeding stock and equipment to raise rabbits for an upcoming chain of fast-food rabbit outlets.

Looking at the map, I can't help but notice how one-dimensional our progress has been. If we ever pass along this narrow thread again, how familiar and historical these roads and towns will seem! But even a few hundred yards to one side of our route, the countryside will be brand new. Why, there's room enough for thousands of bicycle trips across the country, side-by-side and each one completely different!

The rain lets up, and we ride on, making a brief stop in Reynolds, where I catch an item in the local paper. Seems a nearby town, Monon, has been found to have extensive chemical pollution of its groundwater, and the item wasn't even on the agenda of the next town council meeting. Instead they discussed pay raises for city employees, and buying a new mower.

It so happens that Monon (Monon sounds like the name of an industrial waste itself; or maybe the first "n" should be replaced by an "r") is on the twin lakes—Lake Shafer and Lake Freeman—that the

Tippecanoe River formed when it was dammed during the Roaring 20s. They probably don't want to queer the tourist trade. (Compare Ibsen's *Enemy of the People*.)

More rain while we're lunching at the Tree House in Monticello, another resort town next to the twin lakes. Most of Monticello was destroyed by an April 1974 tornado that took eight lives, six of them in a van that was tossed off the Tippecanoe Bridge (which had lots of potholes when we crossed it).

The Tree House is pretty good, despite a lousy salad bar full of creamed and pickled stuff. I had slices of ham rolled around broccoli and cheese, corn chowder, stuffed baker, and homemade cherry pie, with a root beer milkshake. Like the Golden Corrals and Bonanza Steak Houses, you step up and place your order, which is subsequently brought by a server. "Place Order Here—Waitress Service Follows" says the sign over the counter.

Lots of friendly people asking about our trip. Again, we wait out a rainstorm, learning not to get out and ride until the rain's had a chance to subside, resume, then subside again.

It's only raining lightly when we proceed sometime around 3 or 3:30 p.m. From the indication on our state map, we thought we'd enter the Eastern Time Zone at one of these county lines in Indiana, but so far the time hasn't changed. Maybe this state doesn't go on Daylight Savings Time.

US 24 gets busier but fortunately we keep our shoulder, although it sometimes gets waterlogged or gravel-strewn. As we begin to follow the Wabash River, the foliage closes in, and the road dips and curves more. Along the river we could see an old towpath. At one point, about three miles west of Logansport, I stopped to let Nanci catch up, but she didn't come along. After about ten minutes I rode back to find her on the muddy, grassy shoulder pulling off her rear wheel, which had a flat. It was raining lightly, and traffic was moving along pretty fast and close to us. Working together, we speedily patched the tube, which had been punctured by a small rock, and got her back on the road.

Logansport felt like a pretty big town. It must have benefited from the commerce along the Wabash, and it doesn't seem too decayed. We found the Manor Motel towards the east side of town, and since it was well past 6 p.m., decided not to press on to Peru (PAY-roo), another 16 miles. The pleasant Pakistani manager charged us $24 for a clean room with fan and color cable TV. Then he gave Nanci a ride to the laundromat, and I showered and went shopping at a nearby mall for stationery and chain lubricant.

In mid-July Logansport has the Iron Horse Festival, meant to recall the days "when the average American went anywhere—on a business trip or a honeymoon, to the city or to war—by first going down to the depot to catch the steam train," according to a brochure.

They've planned excursions to nearby towns in open window coaches powered by a 1920 vintage locomotive of the Logansport & Eel River Railroad, plus music, an art show, a "Muzzleloader Encampment" of 35-40 units re-enacting 18th and 19th-century lifestyles, and a large competitive display of model railroads. Sounds like fun but neither of us can imagine being here any later in the summer; it's humid enough in early June. Lots of rain while we ate at Wendy's next to the Manor, and we ran back to the room through what seemed like a river in the parking lot.

June 6th   Day 51
69.7 miles
Logansport — Huntington, Indiana

Breakfast at the Holiday Inn. US 24 got busier and narrower till it was positively dangerous, big rigs running both ways, curves and hills, and no shoulders. In Peru the main traffic was routed onto a bigger road so we rode quietly along the former main road to the town of Wabash. Passed some big plants manufacturing containers, then came the narrow streets and old brick houses of the "suburbs" before the town proper. We climbed the hill to the edge of big Highway 24 and had "calizzas" at a Pizza Hut.

Outside the restaurant, my toeclip broke off, so after lunch we rode back to town and found a bike shop, Richard's Sales and Service, on

Market Street (it's always either Market or Main Street in these towns). Ilse Kitchen and her husband received us warmly and offered the best selection of parts and accessories we've seen since Phoenix. I bought a Spenco seat pad and a new Zefal pump in addition to a new pair of toeclips, and Nanci got a little spray can of HALT! for her four-footed antagonists. Ilse told us her daughter has biked across the USA several times, and intends to do it a total of ten times.

Ilse also gives Nanci a better route out of town, to rejoin the Bikecentennial Route at Lagro. What a relief to be back on our little farm roads after busy US 24! The route takes us into the Salamonie State Forest and across a dam, with the wide reservoir to the south and the riverbed running through a gorge to the north. It begins to rain lightly. I'm in my complete rain suit—jacket, pants, booties—and it's cool enough with the headwind and the moisture so we're both nearly comfortable.

Some hills through here—actually just pronounced rising and falling of the road. Still lots of corn and beans and flooded, unplanted fields.

We decided to ride into Huntington for a motel, since we had less than two hours of light, and Fort Wayne, which our route skirts to the south, was still 20 miles ahead. The Hoosier Motel is on the east edge of town, and though a bit overpriced ($27) it's decent enough. The manager seems a bit huffy when I ask to see the room first. Once inside, with our wet gear hung to drip, I pull out Nanci's front tube and patch a slow leak while we watch *Miami Vice, Knightrider,* and *Stingray* on the TV, and order a Domino's Pizza delivery.

June 7th   Day 52
87.5 miles
Huntington, Indiana — Ottawa, Ohio

Light rain the next morning, which slowly dissipates. The sun even pokes through as we stop in Poe for breakfast, served by a funny, talkative guy with a drawling speech and a slight lisp, who seemed gruff at first but gave excellent service, while the locals relaxed on this Saturday morning drinking beer. But we had fried toast, eggs and special sausage, which he says he cooks up for the guys from the GM plant. "I'll ride their bikes the rest of the way and stick 'em with this place," he mugs to the barflies as he presents us with the $6 bill. "Thanks for shopping Poe-mart." It's interesting how our perception of this place changed from a surly bar scene to a friendly, informal cafe.

Coming out of Poe we met a bicyclist heading the other way, from Akron to Oregon. He's my age or a little older, dressed in black, packed with stuff sacks protruding vertically out of his panniers, helmet stuck on one of them. He hadn't been having fun in the rain—still shaking down, I guess.

Continuing into Ohio, clouds gather and we ride into Monroeville just in time to dodge a heavy rainstorm by having a second breakfast of pancakes in the only joint in town that's not a bar, according to the woman running it (her daughter was the waitress).

We're on the Wayne Trace now, a trail traveled by armies under General "Mad" Anthony Wayne and Benjamin Harrison (later President) to and from Fort Wayne. It's flattened out considerably again.

Lots of red brick buildings now, including a huge Catholic church in Glandorf, built in 1834 and seemingly modelled after a European cathedral. There are a lot of Catholic shrines in people's yards, and a lot of German names on the mailboxes.

Over the phone we find out that the campground we'd planned on north of Ottawa is out of business, so we call some motels in town. Just then huge black clouds blow in, and we take timely refuge in a convenience store while a violent thunderstorm drops several inches of rain.

A few miles later in Ottawa, we go to the east end of town, through at least ten traffic lights (for a town of 1500?), and get a $23 room in the Lee-Bell Motel. Nicely decorated, but a little small for us and our two bikes. We planned a walk downtown but it's raining so we eat cheese, fruit and crackers in the room, and later I walk several blocks for some beers. Although there's a color TV, we listen to classical music from Ft. Wayne instead.

"The traveler learns many precious lessons," wrote Cyrus Bartol in his 1855 European travelogue, "but perhaps the most precious of them all . . . is that the crown of life is no change of place, but is to be in one's home."

June 8th   Day 53
82 miles
Ottawa — Fremont, Ohio

Next morning an undistinguished breakfast at the Schnipke Inn, recommended by our motel manager, a tattooed guy who also runs a printing shop in the next town. His wife pours hot coffee in the morning for the guests. He says he hates rain—used to live in Albuquerque and liked it. But we're looking at some sun and big puffy clouds now, and it's kind of cool. After breakfast we stop at the bakery where the baker gives us additional cookies for free, "so you'll remember Ottawa." Mr. Schwartz is white-haired with a white paper cap, white shirt and red suspenders, and his bakery is open six days a week from 6-6 and today, Sunday, from 8-noon.

The wind has shifted from southeast to northwest and is rapidly clearing the clouds away. We have to ride quite a few miles north into it, but compared to the clouds and rain the cool, dry air is welcome from any direction. A woman coming back from church, her kids in the car, offers us water if we ride back to her house. Nice folks everywhere.

The entire Ohio portion of the Iowa-Maine route is signed with little green bicycle symbols, an arrow indicating direction of travel.

Around Bowling Green things looked very suburban. Some Yellow Pages research resulted in a 2-1/2 hour California-style lunch at the Aspen Bar & Grill on East Wooster, near the university: mesquite-grilled fresh marlin, gazpacho, pasta, Bass Ale on tap, gelato, and good coffee. Fresh flower garnishes. Young urban professional heaven.

Ohio is another state with screwy liquor laws—you have to be connected to a 40-bed or more motel/hotel to serve wine or liquor on Sunday. Beer is okay, though. The Aspen assured us that in about a month they'd be able to serve wine on Sunday, so they could offer champagne brunches. Decorated spiffily in pastels, prints, and batik hangings from the vaulted, skylit ceiling.

Full as ticks, we rode the remaining 35 miles to the Broken Paddle Campground south of Fremont on the Sandusky River. Not very quiet, despite its "Family Campground" sign—some drunkenly exuberant folks motoring in the river. Rows of RVs slept on the broad grassy sites, as the suburban traffic hissed by on the road.

Some miles earlier Nanci had gotten a flat on her rear wheel in the best possible location, someone's grassy front yard, the sun low and cool. We put our spare 1-1/8″ tire on with a new tube, since the Cyclepro tire seemed to have at least one hole big enough for pieces of gravel to work their way through. The narrower tire looks a lot better to me as I ride along behind her—faster and less friction.

"Fireflies," said Nanci that night at the campground. "That's how I can tell we're somewhere else."

June 9th   Day 54
95 miles
Fremont — Cleveland, Ohio

Next morning I received a Toledo rock station, warning boaters on this fine, cool, sunny, windy day to beware of floating debris—tires, trees, etc.—in Lake Erie. Breakfast in Clyde, where the largest washing machine plant in the world, Whirlpool, is located. We talk with Mr. & Mrs. Clyde on the small town street about his brain operation and her pet store.

About barns: Seems like they're painted in only two colors: red and white. Or they're left to weather naturally. Some we've seen are emblazoned with owner's name and date of construction, e.g., "Harvey Rosewood, 1903." Lightning rods and ventilators.

The tradition of painting barns red seems to have originated when farmers mixed up red iron oxide, skimmed milk and lime and applied it to their barns. The homemade preservative hardened into a coat like red plastic. Even after more effective "store-bought" potions became available, the custom persisted. And, the color aids in absorbing sunlight to warm the barn during the winter months. (This information courtesy of *Country* magazine.)

We're definitely getting into some older territory now, but still very suburban, as we get closer to Cleveland. The drivers drive faster and more recklessly, and the litter quotient rises. We get yelled at once by some teenagers speeding by on the narrow, potholed road.

Entering Cleveland our map routes us on the Valley Parkway, the "Emerald Necklace" as a gas station attendant calls it. We're riding in a narrow wooded corridor that encircles the city to the south, with a paved bike path most of the way. We have reservations at the Holiday Inn in Middleburgh Heights, off route but the only one that could take us this late in the day.

Nanci meets Phil Kramer biking through the park, a NASA scientist who leads us to the end of the bike path from where we ride two miles along a city boulevard to the Inn.

Phil reported that things haven't slowed down at NASA due to the recent shuttle explosion—they expect to have a prominent role in the coming exploration and settlement of the inner solar system over the coming century.

This evening the park is full of people on foot and bicycles, and at a large lake there's hordes of teenagers, with police busy keeping tabs on them. Even with our loads we seem to be traveling a lot faster than most of the other bikers.

June 10th   Day 55
72.8 miles
Cleveland — Hambden, Ohio

The NASA-Lewis Visitor Center with its extensive exhibits is open but we didn't get to see it. Instead we luxuriated in the Holiday Inn, sleeping in. Nothing like a vacation.

According to the literature in our room there are also plenty of theaters, museums, restaurants, and other cultural attractions. We could stay busy in Cleveland for several days, but we must push on.

Cleveland was founded in the first years of the 19th century by Moses Cleaveland, acting on the suggestion of George Washington. The Shaker Heights suburb was home to the Shaker sect in the late 1700s and early 1800s. They became famous for making furniture, especially straight-backed chairs, but since they practiced sexual abstinence, the sect quite understandably died out.

Yesterday Phil Kramer assured me that Cleveland was on an upswing now; it has the Rock and Roll Hall of Fame, an honor won from Philadelphia and other cities. "They claim all the big acts started out in Cleveland, before they hit Philly and New York," scoffed my brother, a Philly booster. "Sure." Also the town's baseball team, the Cleveland Indians, are supposed to be doing better. I wouldn't know.

Riding out of Cleveland, the rural mailboxes for the *Marion County Messenger* and *Berez Beacon* are replaced by the *Wall Street Journal*. No more working farms, just restored and boutiqued barns. Bad roads, too, chopped up and full of gaping holes—I bet they replace shocks and suspensions on plenty of Volvos and Mercedes's around here. We were weaving and dodging the potholes once we were off the parkway, and back on the now-steep suburban roads.

Chapter Seven:
Lake Country

June 11th   Day 56
37.5 miles
Hambden — Geneva-on-the-Lake, Ohio

Out here by Lake Erie they had an earthquake last February. "Five-something," said Joey, a stocky twelve-year-old on a BMX whom we met at the laundromat in Geneva. No damage, houses just swayed and a few old gravestones fell over. Now there's a flood emergency from so much rain. Roads are closed everywhere—we see loaders cleaning some of them up.

Last night at Paradise Beach Campground outside Hambden we had the park to ourselves, on the grass beside a little lake covered with lily pads. Just as we were ready to get into the tent, it started to rain. We ate our cozy, cold dinner of crackers, cheese, and fruit inside along with two Genesee Cream Ales we'd bought in Chardan. The rain and wind were severe, and this morning I emerged to find my bike toppled by the wind from where I'd leaned it against a picnic table, the bike cover blown off and serving as a pool liner in which my shoes and left pannier were soaking. We rode 30 miles to Geneva, just ahead of a thunderstorm, lunched at Howard Johnson's, and spent a couple hours in the laundromat drying off. Through the window we watched some "severe thunderstorm activity," as the weather channel calls it. The street flooded a foot deep, with fire engines roaring past to a house fire. Joey rode his bike through the water to chase them, returning with his back plastered with mud. We continued talking with the "Dragon Lady," a woman in a kimono who was busy cleaning the place, accompanied by her talkative teenage daughter.

We rode a few miles further to Geneva-on-the-Lake, through some locally-flooded streets. Everywhere there are grapes, acres and acres of them, 70 percent Concord, since they have to withstand hard freezes.

Lake Erie looks green-gray before it melts into the leaden sky. It's very warm and humid until we get right down along the town's strip of motels, resort cottages, fast food and amusement arcades, where a cool wind blows off the water.

After shopping around we settled on Pera's Motel a few blocks off the lake—$25 plus tax for a big two-room efficiency. There are weather warnings up for the next 24-36 hours, heavy rain and flooding.

Times like this—a few hours of daylight left as we get settled, some leisure, like yesterday's slow awakening in the Holiday Inn—make it really seem like we're on vacation. Other times this trip is like a job. Get up, pack, ride 80 miles, stop, eat, sleep. Still, there's more variety in it, more adventure and improvisation, than in the average occupation.

Joey identified the least of our burdens when he asked me, "What's it like, not watching TV for seven weeks?"

We laid out all the damp stuff in our room and went for veal parmigiana at Mary's Home-Cookin' on New Street. We learned that this county, Ashtabula, is "Covered Bridge Country," though we haven't seen one since Illinois. There are many older visitors who come every season, staying at one of the cottages with the screened-in porches. Plenty of younger ones, too, strutting around the dingy little strip with their cut-off t-shirts, smoking cigarettes and acting cool.

After dinner we went shopping for souvenirs and Father's Day cards. One retail clerk, an older woman with missing upper teeth, told us her boyfriend wanted her to move with him to Barstow, California. We told her to do it. She said she was born here, and the gray days around these parts were many, and people's attitudes matched the weather. I wonder what she'll think of the lunar Mojave landscape where she's going, with that inescapable burning sun. She may daydream of cool, wet, gray days.

Coming out of the shop into the dusk, who should we meet but our pal Joey, who'd ridden his bike from Geneva at the behest of Joyce, the Dragon Lady, to get our address. We were knocked out—he'd arrived only a half-hour ago, and was ready to give up. He came over to the room and talked for a few minutes. He has applied some primitive tattoos to himself, apparently with a ballpoint pen.

Geneva-on-the-Lake has the first miniature golf course in the country, built in 1924, but not much night life. It's also clear why our motel was relatively inexpensive: no hot water, and too late to call the manager.

June 12th   Day 57
93 miles
Geneva-on-the-Lake, Ohio — Corry, Pennsylvania

We're standing beneath some roadside trees waiting out a brief but heavy downpour. Then we cross the state border on a county road, which immediately deteriorates. Outside of Cambridge Springs our county roads were closed due to flooding, so we took Route 6, the "Grand Army of the Republic Highway," to Corry. This is the same Route 6 that crosses Nevada and ends in Bishop, California. Busy but well-surfaced, and it leads us to a fruit stand for refreshment.

Outside of Conneautville, some folks shouted to us from their yards, "There's a tornado watch on!" Okay, we're watching. We keep nervously looking over our shoulders, into the wind, waiting for the next downpour from the darkest clouds.

As we were deciding whether to brave the "Road Closed—High Water" sign near Cambridge Springs, a smart-looking young fellow in a Volvo pulled up. A bicyclist, he used to work for the county road department, and helped us figure out a new route. A pickup went by us, past the signs, and stopped, and we realized that the high water covered the road beginning only a few hundred feet from where we were standing.

Downhill into the narrow, hilly streets of Union City, high slanting rowhouses tilted toward each other like in some medieval town. A family of Amish appeared on foot across the railroad tracks by the supermarket, the women in black bonnets and gray dresses, the men in broad-brimmed straw hats, moving warily in a tight group, like scared deer.

Coming into some hills, we saw a side road to a ski area. Long wooded ridges rise above fields of yellow flowers resembling wild mustard or rabbitbrush. White birches begin to appear, and the gullies along the roads are brimful of muddy water.

We've started passing more abandoned farms, some of them with last year's (or the year before's?) corn still standing, ears and all, dried to fossils in the fields. Old automobile skeletons, through which the weeds grow tall. A neon sign in a bar window in Columbus outside of Corry, proclaims "All Legal Beverages." More screwy state liquor laws.

Unbelievably, we've done over 90 miles to Corry, and a few miles further is the motel, none of whose signs say "Motel," just "Michael Angelo's Lounge—Gourmet Dining." That's where we sit down for dinner, virtually the only customers, served by a beefy, inept young guy in a black leather vest. "Can I help youse?"

June 13th   Day 58
36.9 miles
Corry — Allegheny Reservoir, Pennsylvania

Next morning it's still thickly clouded with a light drizzle but the forecast is for clearing, sunny and dry so we're optimistic—even me. Route 6 is busy. We stop at Columbus for breakfast, another ho-hum coffee shop that's evidently a bar most of the time, judging from the odors of beer and cigarettes. It's cool outside.

There are hills now—we're climbing the Allegheny Plateau—up and down, but it's beautiful. Some functioning farms, mostly growing corn.

Lunch in Sugargrove, where ladies come to the table to talk to us. One even sits down and visits. She tells us of two high school kids from Warren who just left to ride to Alaska for Muscular Dystrophy. It makes me feel frivolous for a moment, not having a cause.

There's a long hill from Russell to Scandia, climbing through the woods to some mountain meadows. A nicely graded highway—the Allegheny Reservoir Scenic Parkway—runs down to the turnoff for Red Oak Campground. $2/person, and boy, are they friendly. Lady at the store opens a bottle of Wesson Oil and sells us half. Local strawberries, too, of which we devour nearly a quart with ice cream after our pasta dinner.

We're assigned a spot down in the "primitive area" of the campground, which is otherwise full of RVs, and we get some morning sun.

Chapter Eight:
More Mountains

June 14th   Day 59
65.6 miles
Allegheny Reservoir, Pennsylvania — Lake Rushford, New York

I rise early and go to the back door of the campground's bakery/store where friendly members of what seems to be several different families give me coffee and conversation as they're pulling trays of turnovers and cookies from the oven.

Earliest inhabitants of this area were the Seneca tribe, one of the five that made up the Iroquois Nation, who portaged through here to avoid a big bend in the Allegheny. The first white settlers stopped here because the bend was frozen further down. They made their living with logging,

---

a little oil, and the coal which was discovered in the 1830s and mined for 100 years.

A chief of the Seneca, Cornplanter, gave his name to this route along the valley. George Washington's government made a treaty with them establishing a certain number of square miles as reservation, parts of which were taken from them as late as the 1960s when the Army Corps of Engineers dammed the river. The Seneca name for the reservoir—Kinzua—translates as "perfidy."

Swedes came in to work the logs—they say it's lucky it was winter with snow on the ground when they came, because if they'd seen all the rocks they'd have to move in the spring, they'd have left at once.

It's beautiful riding past the reservoir, once we can see it. The broad waters are contained between high wooded ridges. The entire area was underwater during previous geological eras; later it was scoured by glaciers. There are seashell fossils in ridgetop rocks, but we can't see them from here.

New York State is looking pretty good, with its green hillsides and frequent meadows. The grades aren't bad, though it's definitely hilly; climbs are interspersed by long level or slightly rolling stretches. As we move along the rivers or between the mountains, we look up at what seems to be very steep slopes, but the roads find reasonable ways of getting over or around them. Affluence seems to reign here, and the houses are well-kept. It's amazing: today, Saturday, *everybody's* mowing their lawn.

This region is called the "Southern Tier," after the row of counties along the Pennsylvania border. Buffalo is the major nearby city. The first time on the entire trip we get abusive hollers from a passing car happens just west of Little Valley, while we're climbing a long grade on a broad shoulder; a mini-pickup full of adolescent males yells obscenities first at Nanci, then at me, while squirting us with a water pistol. The US Army's calling you, boys.

Ellicottsville is a ski town, with one blue chairlift going up the green slope on the edge of town. There's a profusion of deliberately quaint cafes and restaurants, somewhat like the resort towns we're used to in the West.

We camped at Rushford Lake, on a grassy hilltop. Our host, Mildred, is a non-stop talker. She showed us some old books she had just bought at auction. "I'm an antique myself, y'know." She told me that the glaciers that moved south stopped just below this point, depositing a lot of gravel. Many of the tilled fields we've passed lately have very stony soil.

We learned the following from park exhibits, roadside markers, and Mildred: The Seneca were the "Keepers of the Western Door" in the Iroquois federation, which also included the Cayuga, Mohawk, Oneida, and Onandaga tribes. Later the Tuscarora came up from present-day Pennsylvania. The Iroquois are known as the "Long House" people, from the shape of their bark structures. The federation was united by none other than Hiawatha, immortalized by Longfellow's drumlike rhythms:

> And the pleasant water-courses,
> You could trace them through the valley,
> . . .
> And beside them dwelt the singer,
> In the vale of Tawasentha,
> In the green and silent valley.
> There he sang of Hiawatha,
> Sang the song of Hiawatha,
> Sang his wondrous birth and being,
> How he prayed and how he fasted,
> How he lived, and toiled, and suffered,
> That the tribes of men might prosper,
> That he might advance his people!

The white woman Mary Jemison was kidnapped from northwestern Pennsylvania with her family by Senecas in 1755. The rest were killed, but the four-foot-two woman was adopted, made to trek to the Genesee country, and was given an Indian name meaning "Two Voices Falling." She married an Indian brave and had many children. More on her later.

The Iroquois played middlemen to the French and British and prospered greatly, but eventually the French were driven out. When the Revolutionary War began, all but one tribe, the Oneida, sided with Britain. Washington sent troops to "pacify" the Seneca; they burned forty villages and much cropland. In 1797 the Iroquois gave away most of their land in the Treaty of Big Tree. They still live on reservations in western New York, and have reportedly adapted well to white culture.

June 15th   Day 60
29.7 miles
Lake Rushford — Letchworth State Park, New York

Kind of cool today with a sun that couldn't quite make it through the clouds. A few sprinkles on our tent this morning—thundershowers are supposed to persist for another day or two. Meanwhile the bees fumble at the roadside wildflowers like a high school boy on a drive-in date.

Following Mildred's suggestion, we rode a short way along the Genesee River through Fillmore to Letchworth State Park. Thirty-five miles south of Rochester, Letchworth is a 15,000-acre park around a 600-foot gorge cut by the Genesee into the shale and sandstone underlying the dense forests. The river roars over three major waterfalls, one 107 feet high.

Philanthropist William Pryor Letchworth (1823-1910) bought the land comprising the park to prevent the gorge being flooded for a covert hydroelectric project disguised as a flood control dam. On his death the land was bequeathed to the state.

The Genesee is New York's second largest river, flowing 120 miles from Pennsylvania north to Lake Ontario, bisecting the Empire State. We topped a rise on the way to Letchworth, and looked down on the Genesee Valley, broad, dotted with farms, flowing out of misty ridges to the south.

Letchworth first saw the gorge in 1858, its slopes scarred by early lumbering efforts. In 1859 he bought a two-story frame house which had been built in 1820 and enlarged in 1850, and named it Glen Iris. It's now a country inn, elaborately decorated with Victorian antiques, situated on the verge of the Middle Falls which thunder in a white sheet visible from our $37 room in the Pinewood Lodge next door.

We ditched our bags in the room and rode ten miles around the park's southern end. The unburdened bikes felt as though they'd fly out of our hands. We rode to the Council Grounds above our lodge, to where Letchworth moved an Iroquois Long House. There is a memorial statue over the remains of Mary Jemison, and across from Glen Iris a museum filled with Indian artifacts.

More on Jemison from the museum exhibits: she was taken, after her kidnapping, to the Ohio Valley, where she lived three years as the wife of a Delaware Indian chief. He remained to hunt when she and two other adopted "brothers" trekked seven months to reach the Genesee Valley, where they arrived barely alive after hiking on foot through rain, snow, and winter winds. Once, on the Sandusky River, they went 75 miles west, out of their way, to procure supplies, only to find the post abandoned and the traders murdered. She never left the Genesee, but died at the age of 90. Exhibits in the museum trace her genealogy forward from her Scotch-Irish parents, who bore her at sea on the way to the New World, to present-day Seneca and white families.

We had a festive, elaborate dinner at Glen Iris, with our first bottle of New York wine. That night in our room, we heard thunder booming through the gorge.

June 16th   Day 61
59.4 miles
Letchworth — Hammondsport, New York

The pavement looked as if it had rained last night, but the sky was mostly clear with a definite haze to it. It's going to be hot, I think.

A beautiful breakfast at the Glen Iris dining room—pancakes and waffles with "pure Wyoming County syrup," and good coffee, with a view of a rose garden through wall-sized glass windows.

We rode with a good tailwind ten miles to Nunda, "Where the Mountains Meet." Then a four-mile climb of East Mountain. Not hard but it is definitely a cooker today. I'm soaked at the summit, where we meet, coming from the opposite direction, Michael from Rhode Island, riding to California. He's a young fellow with a Yankee accent, worried about his money holding out—"I'll just work somewhere for awhile."

He's not following a preplanned route like we are, but finding his way with an oil company map. Doing okay, he says. "So much of this country is two miles up, two miles down."

Across the next valley is another high ridge, and through the haze are visible silos and barns along its summit. In general the tops of the mountains are broad and well-settled.

A long descent into Dansville, which has some nice old brick buildings, and there we pick up Interstate 390, which we parallel for the next 20 miles along a broad valley to Avoca. We stopped at a grocery there for lunch, which included New York State Sharp Cheddar, "Heluva [the brand name] Sharp Cheese," a pint of fresh black cherries, Koko Drop cookies (floury, lardy, perhaps representing the Puritan Dutch heritage of these parts) and a trio of apple fritters.

We crossed the route of the old New York-Erie Telegraph Line, engineered last century by Ezra Cornell, founder of the university of the same name at Ithaca.

From Avoca we climbed on a county road over a hill, past corn and potato fields, and some of the first slums we've seen in this lush woodland, poor folks living in dilapidated mobile homes. A stiff breeze from the southwest seems to be blowing some weather in; the guy sitting in front of the TV repair shop in Avoca said we're in for a big storm. Was he gloating?

On the descent we expected another ten miles to Hammondsport, but suddenly we're passing the Taylor Winery: old, ivy-covered stone buildings on the hill above us to the left, newer industrial complex spreading below us on the right. It was too late to visit, so we rolled the final two miles into Hammondsport and headed straight for a laundromat. While Nanci did the wash, I walked to the town park in my bathing suit and located a motel room on Keuka Lake, the first of the Finger Lakes.

Keuka Lake is one of the western Finger Lakes, 21 miles long and ten miles wide at its forked northernmost extremity. It's only a few hundred feet deep, and enclosed by ridges that tower a thousand feet above its 700 foot elevation.

This little village of a thousand people has restored the town square, and there are viable businesses in its old brick buildings, businesses that seem to fill locals' needs as well as sell antiques to tourists. There is also the Glenn H. Curtiss Museum, honoring an early developer of fixed-wing aircraft designs (the Curtiss biplane, among others), and the town bills itself as "The Cradle of Aviation" (along with Chanute, Kansas and Kitty Hawk, North Carolina and who knows where else?).

After unpacking at the motel we walked over to the lake for a swim. Climbing down off an iron ladder affixed to a short pier, I found the water similar to Tahoe's—numbing but refreshing—so our dips were brief. A storm blew up while we were dressing for dinner, and we walked the few blocks to the square in our rainjackets. The rain got heavier, and the wind blew, knocking over a chalkboard outside the Village Tavern under whose portico we paused for shelter. The owner came out and talked us in by claiming he had the widest selection of local wines in town.

The tavern was panelled in dark wood and very cheerful. Sitting by the window, watching the thundershower, we sipped glasses of white wine—I had Dr. Konstatin Frank's Chardonnay and Nanci tried his Seyval Blanc. With our excellent lasagna we moved on to Bully Hill's Pinot Noir and one of their red table wines. Although it wasn't on the menu, they brought me a dish of fresh local strawberries for dessert.

During dinner the owner came by and in his New Jersey accent gave us a pep talk about the superiority of New York wine over California's, something about the greater acidity of the soil. While the wines were very good, certainly much better than we'd imagined they'd be, the main advantage so far is the price—about half of what we're used to in California.

Back in the room we tried to watch Sondheim's *Sunday in the Park with George*, but the wine, and perhaps the musical, did their work.

June 17th Day 62
24.6 miles
Hammondsport — Watkins Glen, New York

Next morning the weather took a turn for the incredible—sunny, cool, and breezy. We packed and rode to the Crooked Lake Ice Cream Parlor on the square for the local coffee shop scene, then back to Taylor.

We didn't take the tour, but watched their 12-minute movie, which showed mainly how automated production lines, huge machines, and men and women in white coats enable Taylor, US Bonded Winery #1, to make more wine faster than ever before. We could see through an open doorway into the plant, where endless conveyor belts of green gallon jugs were being filled and packed.

The tasting bar offered us their champagne, with Naturel faring best with us just behind Brut. Gold Seal Chardonnay was as good as at Letchworth, and we found their Empire Cream Sherry to be an excellent, nutty effort.

Next stop on our wine-country mini-tour was Bully Hill, a steep three-mile climb up the west shore of the lake. It was quite a different experience from Taylor's—Bully Hill is a homey, quirky winery run by Walter S. Taylor, who cannot use his name on any of his wine, artwork, or poetry. Taylor's ancestors founded Taylor Winery—what Walter S. is fond of calling Taylor Winery #2—and he was a vice-president until April 1970, when he gave a speech in San Francisco denouncing the use of chemical additives in New York wines, and acknowledging that, at least for drinking purposes, California wines were the best. He was immediately fired from the company, but wasted no time starting Bully Hill, which opened on the location of his grandfather's original Taylor winery. He lost a court battle with the Taylor company concerning his use of the name, but got an awful lot of publicity out of it anyway. He draws his own labels, featuring goats, birds, and his own face, with slogans like, "They got my name and heritage, but they didn't get my goat."

We sat in Bully Hill's Champagne Cafe eating a pasta lunch and conversing with two old gentlemen at the next table, who turned out to have an appointment with Walter. One of the men, with a tanned, white-whiskered face, claimed to be the oldest practicing attorney in New York State. Walter was late, "as usual," but when he showed up, the tall, balding, mustachioed proprietor poured wine all around and kept the customers and the staff off balance with a steady stream of deadpan non-sequiturs and bad jokes. We drank his "Workers' Red" table wine, and in return I sketched a label for a bicyclists' wine. When we left, I presented it to him and he took me into the gift shop and gave me a winery T-shirt. I wore it a lot. Smart move on his part.

We tasted some of his wines—Bully Hill, unlike most New York producers, makes some good reds—and got back on the bikes. We did a mail drop at the Hammondsport post office for the usual half-dozen post cards plus a box of our souvenirs, and while Nanci called her office from the phone booth on the town square, I talked with Ruth, a Hammondsport resident for 55 years. "I hope everyone's been courteous to you," she said, and added that she'd allowed some cyclists to camp in her yard, and prepared them breakfast. She was very eager to hear the details of our trip—a regal senior citizen, white-haired with a wooden cane.

The ride to Watkins Glen wasn't far, but we had to climb out of the Keuka Lake basin, a series of several rather steep ascents through rolling farmland. The weather was just incredible, though, and some folks drinking beer in their yard near the top of the last hill shouted encouragement. Sure enough, it was all downhill from there.

Right before the town, we turned at a sign for Watkins Glen State Park, and commenced a steep climb. About a quarter-mile up, a man in a van stopped and explained to us that the sign was misleading; it pointed to the upper entrance to the park, a remote area with no camping. We gratefully rode back down through town, bought some food and beer, then climbed the right hill, up to the park's south entrance. We found a beautiful, dry, campsite among the pines and the oaks, pitched our tent, cooked up dinner and hit the bags.

June 18th   Day 63
47 miles
Watkins Glen — Seneca Falls, New York

Next morning we hiked through part of the Watkins Glen gorge, a deep cut through shale and sandstone laid down 650 million years ago, sliced by a stream coming off the flanks of Sugar Hill. The steep narrow walls were covered with ferns, and little waterfalls sprayed the trail along which we walked, above the stream that snaked through the rock, cutting sinuous passages or cascading in chutes and falls. Stone bridges and walls lined the trails and arched over the gorge. The early sun beamed over us, and the pines perfumed the cool, dry air just like at home in the Sierra Nevada.

The road up the east shore of Seneca Lake wasn't nearly as steep as the one out of Keuka. We stopped at Wagner Winery for a short tour and tasting—some interesting wines but nothing outstanding, except for the Aurora grape juice. They had some typical East Coast varietals such as Vidal, Niagara, DeChaunac, and Rabat.

Our tour guide, Vicki, a college freshman, said she'd often felt like opening her car door in front of a bicyclist, "not to be mean, but just to see what would happen." We convinced her that it would indeed be mean, and felt better when we found out that she lived in the opposite direction from where we were headed.

While we'd been touring Watkins Glen gorge earlier in the day we'd caught glimpses of a figure in an orange bicycling shirt, scampering along the trail taking pictures. We met him on our way up the southeast shore: a 62-year-old man from Willow Grove, Pennsylvania, cycling from his home to Bar Harbor, Maine. Wiry, energetic, fast-talking in a Philly accent, he boasted of bicycling a total of 11,000 miles last year. His son got him into cycling at age 52, and now he's an official in a local bike club. I took his picture and he sped off, no doubt to do 120 miles before dark.

Somewhere here in upstate New York, this bicycle trip has really gotten into gear. It's difficult terrain, but we're stoic and unrelenting on the numerous uphills, stable on the descents, and grateful for the good weather. Pounding away the miles has become second-nature as we pay more attention to the scenic, historic and cultural treats that unfold around us.

And this kind of life, in general, is so exhilarating because it's so streamlined: our problems are very basic, our lifestyle quite simple. We can find happiness in a smooth road, a cool breeze, a hot meal, a cold beer.

As we proceed north along enormous Seneca Lake, the terrain gets gentler, as if when the glaciers ground into the high plateau to make these big lakes, they sanded down this lower area into smoother rolling hills. The north end of the lake also seems more settled; there are still farms but also some fine old homes behind big lawns. When we turn and go down to ride along the lakeshore there's a seaside smell in the air, and prosperous-looking Cape Cod-style homes with late-model sedans in the driveways.

To one who's spent the last 15 years west of the Rockies, amid sparser, more specialized vegetation, this is like riding in a tropical rain forest: greenery thickly mats the rocky ground, and vines crawl along fences and walls. But I know why it's so green—the Eastern sun is congenitally unable to shine more than two days in a row. It's bound to rain sooner rather than later. Although we won't like it, the buttercups, clover, and gorgeous orange lilies will be glad.

We're following in reverse, here and there, the route of Generals Clinton and Sullivan on their 1779 mission of pacification to the British-backed Seneca Indians. Their longer-range purpose, to clear the area for further settlement, has evidently succeeded.

The dates we're seeing on buildings and historical monuments are mostly from the early 19th century, with a few from the late 18th century. We pass a big mansion, Rose Hill, just west of Geneva. Tall white Doric columns are the backdrop for a huge lawn surrounded by a wrought-iron fence with decorative flourishes. Built in 1820, the estate's economy was agriculturally-based, and an early proprietor developed the first ceramic tile drainage system for his fields.

We crossed into Waterloo, a small industrial city where the Cayuga-Erie canal, with its brand new shiny locks, is still in operation. Deciding to use our last Holiday Inn scrip, we check into one near Seneca Falls, and pay the full rate ($49) for their last vacancy, a converted meeting room with sofa bed. Very uncomfortable, even though we took the mattress off the sofa and put it on the floor.

June 19th   Day 64
87.4 miles
Seneca Falls — Pulaski, New York

Next morning black clouds defaced the western sky. We rode into Seneca Falls, site of the first Women's Rights Convention in 1848 and birthplace of suffragists Amelia Jenks Bloomer and Elizabeth Cady Stanton. Big old vacant mills lined the river, with beautiful mansions along the side streets. Like Rose Hill, the cubical homes are capped by a smaller cubical turret, usually glassed-in. Lots of brick and stone everywhere.

Riding north through the Montezuma Wildlife Refuge, we saw a white-tailed deer bounding off the road. Here also are drumlins, tiny (10-50 ft. high) tadpole-shaped hills left by the glaciers, formed when the upper layers overrode the rock-laden lower layer. Between them the ground is getting swampy. On the high ground they're still growing corn.

Saw an old fellow, obviously a basement inventor, sitting in the shade of his barn door holding a unit that remotely controlled his lawnmower, connected to him by a cable as it buzzed about his lawn. He grinned when he saw us.

Since Little Valley, anywhere we've been over 1000 feet above sea level there've been wild strawberries by the roadside. Seems like they'd be loaded with lead from passing auto exhausts, so we haven't indulged. But they're everywhere.

Lunch at Fair Haven, not exactly on Lake Ontario but on Little Sodus Bay. While our bikes rested against a tree in the light rain, we had soup and sandwiches at the Mt. Pleasant Hotel. This yacht club flies both Canadian and American flags, and has a nice dining room, very Eastern in its conservative decor. Next to us are seated a couple of white-haired guys in blue blazers and rep ties, drinking highballs and swearing mildly while their tanned, husky-voiced wives sulkily smoke long cigarettes.

From there we cut across to Fulton, on the Oswego River. The Seaway Trail was closer to the lake, and might have been more scenic, but we figured it would be busier. Fulton was another old mill town, with huge brick and stone structures by the river. Heavy traffic both in and out of town until we got off the state highway and on county roads, which took us north to the towns of Mexico and Texas (one roadside restaurant was called the Texas Cookhouse, "Our Specialty Texas Hots"). Late in the afternoon, right before Port Ontario, we met some clean-cut, friendly teenagers at the Dairy Whizz. The older guy (my age) who joined us for a few minutes, stepping out of his van where a woman waited ("Bet you guys took plenty of pot along," he said to us), came off as positively sleazy in comparison to these all-American high school kids. One girl thought that bike touring would be "the neatest thing. I'm going to marry a guy who likes to do that."

Pulaski lived up to its name: a rough-looking Polish mill town, the Ontario Iron Works dominating the south end. Across the interstate was the Redwood Motel, where we were directed by a kindly barmaid in town. A good deal—$27 for a nice room. That night the dark clouds that had loomed to the south delivered, and it rained very hard, with fireworks. We sat inside, eating leftover pizza and watching *Trapper John MD*, guest-starring our cross-country media companion, Hoyt Axton.

Chapter Nine:
More Familiar Faces

June 20th   Day 65
80.6 miles
Pulaski — Nick's Lake, New York

The weather cleared the next morning for our ride into the foothills of the Adirondacks. Less and less settlement lined the secondary roads, as we wound deeper into the woods, passing a beautiful blue lake with no marks of habitation at all. We saw signs for a cheese factory, but when we passed it the cottage-type establishment was closed. We had expected big grades through here but there were none, just gradual step-like climbs and some descents. At West Leyden we crossed the Mohawk River a half-mile below its source. A ruined old factory stood beside some low falls created by a crumbling dam.

In Boonville, a busy little village, we lunched at the imposing Hulbert

House, built in 1803 by Ephraim Owen. Natural limestone walls and tall white columns give it an air of old-fashioned elegance, and it was hard to visualize it standing when Indians traversed the narrow trails eastward towards the rich mountain hunting grounds. This is called the Highmarket region, drained by the Black River, whose valley lies between those of the Mohawk and the St. Lawrence. In the 19th century the Black River Canal & Railroad used Boonville as its northern terminus, causing an economic boom in the area, as lumber and furs were shipped downstream, and trade goods upstream.

The house in which we lunched was bought in 1840 by state legislator Richard Hulbert, and it became famous for its genial proprietor and plentiful meals of venison, steak, and speckled trout. Famous customers included Horace Greeley, William F. Cody, U.S. Grant, New York governor Thomas Dewey, and Franklin Delano Roosevelt.

These days the food is good but ordinary—sandwiches, some fried stuff, and excellent fresh peach shortcake—and our aging waitress was of the old-fashioned slow but polite school. The decor was of a comparable vintage; the current owners have stripped away layers of paint, wallpaper and cheap panelling to reveal the authentic early 19th-century woodwork.

After Boonville we crossed the Black River and climbed a ridge into an unexpected stand of skinny lodgepole pines, less than half as thick as their Western cousins. We caught the smell of the mountains—clean, dry, and resinous.

Aluminum soda and beer cans here have the printed legend   5 CENT DEPOSIT NY VT ME MA CT.   We have noticed almost no roadside litter in New York. No cans, no bottles. We're even hard-pressed to spot a cigarette butt.

It's Friday, early evening, two weeks before the Fourth of July, but traffic's not overwhelming yet. Generally good shoulders on the road into the Adirondack Forest Preserve, which begins inconspicuously right after Woodgate. Still plenty of private property, which we understand is controlled by the state with regard to tree-cutting and new construction. Kenneth Nash's book *Wilderness and the American Mind* tells among other interesting things how the Adirondack Preserve was created: in 1885, when increased deforestation of upstate New York had caused enough erosion to taint New York City's water supply, the Empire State set aside the region as a future metropolitan water supply. I also heard that there was a titanium mine here during World War II.

Tackle shops, canoe rentals, restaurants, motels, little groceries in the pines—we must be in the resort village of Old Forge. A few miles' ride around McCauley Mountain brings us to Nick's Lake, where all the lakeside campsites are taken, but there are plenty of other wooded spots. Nanci and I sign in and get settled, and a few hours later Dick and Ed Fenimore show up, showing true brotherly devotion, or else uncontrolled ambition to go a-fishin', by driving seven hours from Philadelphia to meet us.

Except for a few media personalities, theirs are the first familiar faces we've seen since Roger rode away that morning in Flagstaff. After pitching our three tents we go into town for a late dinner of steak, brews, and conversation, then return to camp and hit the bags.

June 21st   Day 66
A Day Off In the Adirondacks

Next morning, sunny and warm, we move to a beautiful, newly-vacated site right on the lakeshore, and rent a couple of canoes. The day is spent idly drifting on the lake, and late in the day Ed catches a 15″ brown trout, which the ranger tells us is one of 30,000 extra dumped in Nick's because there was nowhere else to put them.

Dick has brought us a present: two nice Fuji touring tires which I put on our front wheels, as the ones we've ridden on since the start are looking cut up and frayed on the sidewalls.

After many Rolling Rocks we cook spaghetti, beefing up the Ragu sauce with Italian sausage and vegetables. We don't stay vertical for much longer after that.

June 22nd   Day 67
43.1 miles
Nick's Lake — Lake Durant, New York

Next morning is cloudy. Nanci and I ride, sans panniers, to Blue Mountain Lake, then three miles south to Lake Durant. Once again, like at Letchworth, the bikes are so light we feel as if we could climb trees. I'm riding just a few miles from the entrance to Durant when I hear a scraping sound on my front fender. It's a classic flat, the broadheaded roofing nail protruding dead center from my brand-new tire. I sit on the grassy embankment to patch it, Dick and Ed pausing at one point to offer encouragement and a cold Rolling Rock. At the lake we have our pick of sites, so we choose the most spectacular one, on the shore looking across at 3700' Blue Mountain. Dick and Ed rent another canoe, which is delivered to our site by a couple of young kids in a station wagon.

That afternoon Nanci and I go for a ride across Lake Durant, circumnavigating a tiny island and cruising past numerous lily pads with flower buds about to burst. A beaver splashed into the water. The sky grew gray and a light wind picked up.

Our little dam-building buddies were one thing the Algonquin Indians hunted when they took to the Adirondacks. White Europeans didn't actually penetrate the region until the late 18th century, and the railroads didn't come in until nearly 50 years later. By then, besides lumber and pelts, the mountains were producing talc, tin, garnet, zinc, and iron ores.

By the 20th century highways were built, opening the way for automobiles (and bicycles). The main roads offer no ungodly steep grades, which is due not to any great feats of civil engineering, but to the fact that these mountains are ancient, even by geologic standards, and therefore relatively gentle and rounded. Also, the roads generally follow watercourses and the shores of large lakes when possible.

Dick and Ed try their hand at fishing when Nanci and I return in the canoe, but it's early yet. We dress and drive to Long Lake, 11 miles north, for some inexpensive but pretty good food at the Cobblestone Inn. The place had been recommended by Durant caretakers Mr. and Mrs. Guarlick, a voluble older couple who've lived all their lives around here.

After dinner, we retire to the adjoining lounge for some games: foosball, shuffleboard, and ping-pong. The bar is cavernous and we have it pretty much to ourselves.

Back at camp we light the lantern and a fire, but the mosquitoes are numerous and persistent. Ed decides that "mosquito" is an obscene expletive in some Indian language. We climb into our tents for relief from the insects, if not from the humidity. At about three in the morning, rain begins to patter on our tent fly. Soon it's pouring.

June 23rd   Day 68
78.2 miles
Lake Durant — Ticonderoga, New York

By the dawn's light I can see a few mosquitoes outside the tent, slamming themselves against the mesh in a desperate attempt to drink our blood. By seven a.m. the rain has mostly stopped, except for what the wind shakes out of the trees. A heavy fog hangs over the lake, obscuring all but the faintest outline of the opposite shore. Soon there's coffee, and we make desultory conversation while standing beneath the open hatchback, not relishing the current state of our environment.

By the time Nanci and I have our bikes packed, and the brothers are ready to depart, the wind has cleared enough of the sky so the sun's blazing through. It's turned into a sunny, if humid, day.

Dick and Ed drive south, and Nanci and I ride up the grade north to the Adirondack Museum, but it costs $6 to enter this renowned complex of exhibits, which we'd have only an hour or so to examine. So, after answering the usual questions from an array of visitors, we take a quick look at a wooden sailboat preserved under a plastic dome, then continue riding the rolling road, an "Award-Winning Environmental Highway," according to the sign, to Long Lake, for lunch at the Village Inn. The waitress is another of the "Oh, I'd love to do that" types, and we try to talk her into a ride to Maine, with her mother driving her two young children in the sagwagon.

I like her attitude better than "You guys are crazy," or "I like my Ford," or the depressing "Gee, I wish I was young." We attempt to stress to these enthusiastic people that while conditioning is important, it's not the ruling factor in such an endeavor; planning and equipment are more crucial, and of course determination is the overriding necessity. Start with some long dayrides, Nanci counsels her, then try an overnighter.

We've decided that we liked the previous day's arrangement of having Dick carry the gear in his Bronco and supply me with a beer while I was patching the flat. For our next trip, possibly on the TransAmerica Trail from Astoria, Oregon to Denver, Colorado, we'll try to find some compliant soul who enjoys reading or fishing and driving the support vehicle.

Our progress through the heart of the Adirondacks seems amazing to me. The brisk wind is mostly at our backs, and there are no long or steep hills. Just past Newcombe a vast panorama of peaks is revealed on our left, including, I imagine, Mt. Marcy, since a sign informs us we're on the Roosevelt-Marcy Highway. The peaks are pineclad right to their summits, with occasional cliff bands or long streaks of light rock protruding through the dark blue foliage.

Soon after this we leave the main road when it curves south, and get on the Old Blue Ridge Road. We've already crossed the Hudson River (on the road between Blue Mountain Lake and Durant we crossed from the Lake Champlain to the Hudson River drainage) and now we climb, by easy steps, back over to Lake Champlain's territory. The Adirondacks drain into five major systems: the Hudson River, the St. Lawrence River, the Mohawk River, Lake Ontario, and Lake Champlain.

This road is lightly travelled and nearly uninhabited, running through unbroken stands of spruce, birch, cedar and pine. There's a tiny bit of logging and we see a few trucks, but not many. As we gain elevation the trees seem to become shorter, and I really feel as if we're gaining altitude. Since we're at about 2000 feet elevation on the road, and the mountains are another 2000 feet higher, there's plenty of relief to the landscape. Occasional outcrops of granite stand by the road. Somewhere near here, I found out later, is the Balancing Rock, an immense boulder perched precariously on a ledge by ancient glaciers. It's near the Boreas River, a mile to one side or the other, perhaps not far off the road at all.

A couple miles of descent and we're at I-87, the Adirondack Northway. Some of the motels and resorts along here, and along US 9 to the south, look to be in trouble, battered and closed up tight. Maybe their season hasn't yet begun (school's just ending for New York kids) or maybe it's too tough and short a season to offset the slack times.

The surface of US 9 is slightly deteriorated and there's some high-speed rural traffic headed for Schoon Lake (we're riding along the Schoon River, Adirondack ridges above us to the west) so we're glad to turn east on State 74. Glad, that is, till we come to a six-mile stretch of roadwork. We ride through gravel and sand, walking our bikes for the worst 200 yards, nearly as far as Eagle Lake. The resorts look healthier here, along the shores of this nice granite-rimmed lake. To our right, signs proclaim a wilderness area, with trails. Greenery has risen back up to encase the road—we're losing altitude fast now.

After a well-graded two-mile climb, what a sight there is to see: far below us, the valley of Lake Champlain, and the historic city of Ticonderoga. Beyond it, the Green Mountains of Vermont. All of this lit in the golden light of the setting sun.

It's an exhilarating 2.5-mile descent into Ticonderoga, where we take a break from camping at the Stone House Motel on Montcalm Street, next to the Hancock House (an exact replica of the one in Boston), $35 a night and nice. It's an old tourist home from the 20s, done in Tudor. Our room is upstairs, behind a heavy wooden door, and there's a big common living room and veranda. They've seen plenty of bikers. In fact, some of them blew it for us by working on their bikes in their room and getting grease on everything, so we're not allowed to take the bikes into our room, but lock them in the musty old basement instead.

Fort Ticonderoga was built by the French in 1755 on a rocky promontory overlooking Lake Champlain and the Green Mountains beyond. This star-shaped stronghold was attacked six times and held successfully on three of those occasions. French General Montcalm's army of 3500 defended it against Abercrombie's 13,000 Englishmen during a battle of the French and Indian War in 1758; a few years later retreating Frenchmen destroyed it but the British rebuilt it in time for the Revolutionary War. Ethan Allen may have been a lout and a braggart, as someone once said, but he will live in history as the man who led a ragtag band of 83 Vermonters—the Green Mountain Boys—on the successful Ticonderoga raid of 1775, surprising the sleeping garrison and capturing it. Later in the war General Henry Knox took the fort's cannons to Boston to aid General Washington; America's first navy, commanded by Benedict Arnold, was outfitted here; Burgoyne commanded the outpost before he left for Saratoga and it was never garrisoned again; and Washington made a final visit to "Fort Ti" in 1783.

The ruins were restored by the Pell family in 1908, and their descendants are still actively involved in managing and expanding the visitor facilities, which include large collections of Colonial and Revolutionary guns. During the summer tourist season, costumed militiamen explain the exhibits and stage demonstrations of cannon-firing and other military activities. Fife and drum music echoes off the stone redoubts much as it did during the 18th century.

I'm excited, not so much by all the history around us, but by our pending immersion in New England.

Chapter Ten:
Civilization Ho!

June 24th   Day 69
40.0 miles
Ticonderoga, New York — Rochester, Vermont

Next a.m. is sunny but dark clouds loom to the west over the furry Adirondack ridges. We're in a hurry to meet the ferry so it's a quick breakfast of doughnuts and orange juice in the motel parking lot while the bikes are repacked, upon which I discover my rear tire has lost half of its air. I decide to postpone dealing with it, pump it up, and we ride through town, across the LaChute River, past the fort and out to the Vermont Ferry, which runs continuously during the daylight hours of May-November. As it approaches our side, I see old Tahoe pal Ramsey, his son Chris, Karen, and Tracy all standing on board. Waiting with us to board are two other women, bicycle tourists, doing a loop from Boston, where they attend college, through Massachusetts and Vermont.

We pay our fare of a dollar each and enter Vermont. It doesn't seem like a lot to pay for such a beautiful ride over the sparkling water, even though there's free bridges some distance in either direction. I'm reminded for some reason, though, of a line in Twain's *The Innocents Abroad*: when charged $7 for a paddle across the Red Sea, the author remarks, "No wonder Jesus walked."

The day has grown warm and humid, and it looks like we'll get some rain sooner or later. We put our packs in Ramsey's car, which Karen will drive to Rochester, and pedal down the road, all four of us, heading for the Green Mountains rising above us to the east.

We pass more silos and fields, planted in corn and strawberries, but much smaller operations compared to those in the Midwest. These farms are compact, neat, and picturesque. On the roads here in Vermont we see more and more imported automobiles, especially Volvos and Saabs. Prosperity is in the air.

We've decided to go the way Ramsey recommends, via Brandon Gap

(2170 ft.), rather than our mapped route through the busy college town of Middlebury and over Middlebury Gap. It's about ten miles shorter, too.

On the way we pass Karen and Tracy picking strawberries at a farm, and later they catch up with us and pull over so we can gorge ourselves on the ripe delights, trays of which fill the back of the Volvo. The two bike tourists from Boston, with whom we've been playing leapfrog along the road, stop and eat some too.

The sky gets really black and there's some rain, but not too heavy. I keep pumping my rear tire but finally it's time to repair it, at the base of the final steep section on Brandon Gap. The mosquitoes and black flies provide steady low-grade torture as I find I must not only change the tube, but the tire as well, both of which are cut up pretty badly by the gravel picked up in the tread.

At the summit the rest of the crew is waiting, looking up at cloud-banded Mt. Horrid, which displays a steep cliff of ancient rock. It's cloudy, wet, and cold up here, but to the west, far below, the sun illuminates the lowlands we've just crossed and the dark-green Adirondacks beyond narrow Lake Champlain.

Descending into warmth and occasional sun, we're in the mountains now, following the White River through steep-walled valleys past occasional farms. The well-maintained roads don't carry too much traffic, at least today. If this were the autumn "leaf-peeping" season there would be less room for us, I'm sure.

Artistic Woodworks, Ramsey's business in the village of Rochester, is housed in an old white wooden-frame building with an office on the first floor and living quarters on the second. In the adjacent barn is the shop, where partners Lance and Jimmy work on signs and doors. The house is reminiscent of Ramsey's former Tahoe residence on Chipmunk Street in Kings Beach with its rudimentary, "collegiate" furnishings, assorted New Age information posted on the walls, a wealth of herbs and grains in the kitchen, and constant company. Karen has her daughter Katy, and watches Lito and Danny while their mother commutes to Boston three days a week to work as an airline stewardess. Tracy lives in the back room, and she's driving to Boston for a few days, so Nanci and I will use her room. The gang empties many bottles of imported beer as Karen fixes pasta salad, fresh bread, and gazpacho. Afterwards we go to the Youth Hostel where Ramsey shows his slides of skiing the Haute Route, from Chamonix to Zermatt.

Ten of the town's few thousand residents are from Tahoe—rather, they've lived in Tahoe for at least a season: Ramsey, Chris, Lance, Jimmy, Doon and his wife Patty, Tracy, and a few more. Rochester is a small town, clean and white against the green hills. It offers at least three bed & breakfast inns, a youth hostel, and a nouvelle cuisine restaurant. The grocery carries an excellent selection of cheeses and wines, including Bully Hill.

There's a definite contrast between the native and immigrant Vermonters—the former, to put it politely, are more inclined to behave in a rural manner. Jimmy is at the opposite end of the cultural spectrum; he lives just out of town, in North Hollow, with a community called Quarry Hill. Leftovers from the 60's, Ramsey calls them. It's evidently some sort of a commune, made up of a close cluster of houses none of which have any siding, since to finish a house would mean they'd have to pay property taxes. We hear the members have an "intense social scene."

June 25th Day 70
A Day Off In Vermont

A month before we began this journey, Nanci spent several long evenings researching the mapped routes, identifying likely campsites, and sketching out on the computer a rough itinerary for the time we had to spend, listing each day's projected mileage and destination. We haven't followed this plan very closely, but at least we have an idea of how far ahead or behind schedule we are—i.e., how many days we have to burn. All along the trip we've been trying to save days or make up lost ones in order to have a few off in New England. Letchworth was a virtual day off. Nick's Lake was another. Today is our fourth full day off since Phoenix, unscheduled yet anticipated, a day of rest, recuperation, and recreation in long-awaited Vermont, and here we are spending the morning in intensive bike maintenance on the Artistic

Woodworks porch, getting greasy amid piles of tools and parts.

Later in the day Ramsey, Chris, Nanci and I drive to Montpelier, about an hour away. On the way we stop in Granville, at a store called Vermont Only, to send some gifts to the folks back home. Then we pause in Warren for some elegant little lunch items.

It's a sunny day, but cold and windy with temperatures in the low 60s. Besides the amounts of precipitation, Vermont weather reports give its pH, which is generally acidic, thanks to the Great Lakes industry upwind.

Montpelier is a beautiful old city, clean and well-maintained. Unlike most of the big towns we've seen during the past few months, there's no gutted or boarded-up buildings that we can see, just prosperous small businesses. As in most big towns, there are a few old stone churches.

Although we've passed plenty of farms, and a couple of wood products plants, Vermont's economy, according to Ramsey, is based on a proliferation of cottage industries such as computer software, crafts, and light manufacturing (Artistic Woodworks is a combination of these last two types). The tourist industry is strong, too—we've passed dozens of bed & breakfasts, and bought croissants, brie, and french roast coffee in the little shops. And whoever is responsible for promoting Vermont as a recreational destination has somewhat whimsically adopted a stylized black and white dairy cow as the informal state mascot.

We go to Onion River Sports for bicycle tires and accessories. Ramsey and Chris are going to ride with us to Maine, and we've convinced Chris to ride his dad's mountain bike. Apropos of nothing (save perhaps Ramsey's feet), Onion River Sports has been written up in the *Wall Street Journal* for a contest they sponsor to pick the nastiest old tennis shoes.

Dinner at the Huntington House, next to Artistic Woodworks, with Ramsey and Karen. They announce plans to move to Nevada City in mid-July, where Ramsey will take over his late father's house on Grove Street and make his signs there. Our dinner is quasi-nouveau, good in conception but faulty in execution. Grilled chicken with an undetectable raspberry sauce, rabbit crepes, baked trout covered in oats, and blackened redfish. The wines were Beringer Chardonnay (good) and Fetzer Fume Blanc (too sweet). Picky, picky. Nice atmosphere, though, like a private dining room in an old inn, and absolutely no other customers.

Walking home later that night we're buzzed by guys driving at high speed through Rochester's village green, honking and whistling like the river rats in Hannibal. These are the aforementioned genuine locals, not the enlightened, long-term tourists, and this an example of what I mean by "behaving in a rural manner."

June 26th   Day 71
50.0 miles
Rochester, Vermont — Lyme, New Hampshire

Next day the four of us set off down the White River towards Maine. Fried clams and chicken salad for lunch at Tozier's, a vintage roadside stand. We didn't leave Rochester until noon, after a cloudless morning, and now big black clouds threaten rain.

Leaving the river at North Royalton, we climb over to Thetford, founded in 1761. East Thetford is right on the Connecticut River, which we cross and follow upstream for a few miles to Wilder Lake Campground, near Lyme and just a few miles north of Hanover, home of renowned Dartmouth College. We're in a nice campsite right on the river, hosted by a fat, beer-smelling guy with a strong New Hampshire/Boston accent, who advises us to continue hanging our food. $4.50/person and we each feed a quarter into the shower machine.

That evening, eating our ramen and vegetable dinner, with a jalapeño cheese bread round and six-pack of Pabst, we heard somebody (the host?) alternately playing old swing tunes on an organ and a tenor sax, reverberating from inside a big metal building on the hill.

That night it rained hard, letting up a few hours after dawn.

June 27th   Day 72
42.01 miles
Wilder Lake Campground — North Woodstock, New Hampshire

Next day another late morning start, and we ride north through the upper Connecticut River Valley for 20 miles, through Haverhill, a beautiful New England town with big white black-shuttered homes, some built before 1800, lined up along the white-fenced village green. The riverside going is flat, unlike the more mountainous terrain around it, and the Valley of the Connecticut is fertile—a glacier ground through it way back when, creating some rich soil. The valley also served as a conduit for settlement, like a pre-industrial interstate.

Lunch is at a biker's dream spot, the Village Bakery and Pancake House in Benton. After doing it justice, we climb 12 percent grades in a light rain to an 1800' summit at Lost River. Beaver Lake is there, as well as an Appalachian Trail crossing below dense foggy clouds overhanging the peaks. We pause to don full armor for our plunge into the Pemigewasset River Valley and the North Woodstock/Lincoln resort area.

North Woodstock is a real four-season resort town. Early inhabitants struggled to hang on with logging and subsistence farming until the millions of inhabitants of the lower industrialized areas of Maine, New Hampshire and Massachusetts realized that here was a very accessible mountain paradise; as a result, as early as the mid-19th century tourism was a significant part of the local economy. It's the primary reason we found a wide selection of restaurants, gift shops, campgrounds, and motels this rainy evening.

Deciding to go whole hog, so to speak, we went into an expensive-looking eating house, where the Friday night special was two one-pound live lobsters for $12.95, with potato salad $1 extra. We had ourselves some beers and behaved boisterously as the tables turned over around us (restaurant jargon).

Next to us sat a Jewish couple from Boston, with their beautiful dark-eyed eight or nine-year-old boy. Both parents are identically short and project a similar well-to-do aura. The father gushed over our trip—he said he was headed to Arizona for a retreat with his "salami" (swami). Pointing to us, Mom said to her son Jason, "You've got to get out and do that, Jason."

Outside after dinner, Nanci's rear tire is flat, so we change it in the dark and the drizzle, with Jason out to watch "in case the same thing happens to my bike." Since the tube is punctured on a seam next to the valve, I replace it rather than patch it. Then we ride in the dark a third of a mile back to Maple Haven Campground.

This place is run by wisecracking, friendly kids in their 20s. It's a big grassy meadow with lots of RVs and car campers already in place this weekend evening. We're on a damp plot right next to a big pond.

June 28th   Day 73
37.2 miles
North Woodstock — Conway, New Hampshire

Sure enough, next morning the black flies and skeeters are out. Coffee from Ramsey's little espresso pot makes them easier to bear as I write four postcards before anyone's up.

Riding through Lincoln, we learn that compared to the more respectable North Woodstock this was formerly the wrong side of the tracks, where the French Canadian loggers lived; now it's all fast food, condos, and ski shops, presenting a familiar aspect to those of us from Sierra resort communities.

Looming 2000-3000' above us are the forested White Mountains. Our route is east, climbing the Kankamagus Highway over Kankamagus Pass (2871'), opened in 1959.

This twisting highway (the "Kank" to locals) is named after Kancamagus (the Fearless One), grandson of Passaconaway, who in 1684 succeeded his uncle Wonalancet as third and final Sagamon of the Pentacook Confederacy. He tried to keep peace between whites and Indians, but continued harassment by the British inflamed his hot temper and led to war. In 1691 the tribes of the confederacy scattered, and Kank with his followers moved to northern Maine.

The climb is on a good road, with a 9 percent grade for the final two of five miles. It doesn't seem too difficult, and the birch trees lining the road are beautiful.

At the summit and just below it to the west are some scenic turnouts, full of vacationers. We learn about *wangans,* or loggers' caches, small deposits of gear and supplies stashed at a site where cutting is to be done. The word derives from French trapper usage: *wanigan,* a borrowed Indian word for their bateaux.

Then it's down the Swift River, a long, fast 15-mile drop toward Conway. We stop at Passaconaway for a picnic lunch at a little park set up around the George House, where we read a story about the ill-fated Colbrath couple. Priscilla Colbrath's husband walked out the front door of this little cabin in 1889, saying he'd be "back in a while." She left a light in the window every night for 39 years, while he apparently gallivanted around Cuba, Panama, and California. When he finally returned his wife had been dead for three years, having lived as a lonely hermit.

Their restored cabin sits amid birches in the shadow of Mount Chocorua, named after an Indian of the late 1700s, whose son frequented the home of a white man, Cornelius Campbell. The boy was accidentally poisoned one day, but Chocorua didn't believe it was an accident, so he killed Campbell's family in revenge. Campbell tracked Chocorua and shot him on the mountain's summit, but not before Chocorua pronounced a curse on the local whites. Evidently he knew what he was doing, because a hurricane swept the Swift River Valley soon afterwards, levelling everything along its half-mile wide path. Later all the cattle died (from a mysterious disease called "Burton Ail," which turned out to be caused by excess lime in the water). As a result, human habitation in the area dwindled.

These days plenty of traffic streams through Conway, another resort town. At the market we meet members of a Bikecentennial Maine-Erie trip, eighteen cyclists of widely-varying abilities and pocketbook sizes. Talking to them, we don't get the impression they're having fun. We were planning on staying at a campground southeast of town, but find out that the tour is staying at one a mile north that costs half as much. They're planning on resting for a day before tackling the Whites. Their leader, Bob, looks like a former military man: impeccable grooming, reserved manner, and a small looseleaf book filled with organized rows of tiny precise writing. We tell them about the road ahead of them. I can't imagine travelling in their direction; we're so glad to be getting into the high country and nearer the coast, while they're heading back toward the soggy, industrialized Great Lakes.

Sometimes, talking to the friendly folks we meet along the road and in campgrounds, I feel like we're proselytizing for bicycle tourism. We sure get a lot of mileage out of describing the three older men on bicycles we've met.

But members of this Bikecentennial tour seem strangely low-key, even the leader and his sidekick, Lou Gottlieb, big black-bearded fellow who rides cleanup to take care of all the mechanical difficulties. Doing the laundry, walking back and forth along the dirt drive through the campground, I pass their fires and hear them murmuring. Ramsey, Nanci and I wash our dinner down with a few Beck's beers, and Ramsey rides back into town for more.

June 29th   Day 74
60 miles
Conway, New Hampshire — Turner, Maine

Next morning is beautiful, and we pack and ride back into town for a mediocre Sunday brunch at the Cinnamon Tree. What's billed as the best coffee in the (Mount Washington) Valley turns out to be totally undistinguished. The rest of the valley must be drinking some bad brew.

From a wide choice of Sunday papers we choose the *Manchester Union-Leader,* and slowly I realize that this was the sounding board for the late, furiously conservative William Loeb, whose wife Nackey now runs the newspaper. We read columns by William F. Buckley and Jeane Kirkpatrick, *Dick Tracy* instead of *Doonesbury,* and an editorial in favor of the South African government's draconian security measures.

Mostly level roads brought us quickly into Maine, past fields of strawberries and potatoes, and even some corn, which I've decided is the most popular crop in the US. Here it's only shin-high at this time of the year.

Folks are rafting, canoeing, and tubing on the Saco River which runs broad, smooth, and clear from Conway into Maine along our route. Once we leave the river's course the terrain begins to roll, reminding us more and more of the Missouri hill country. This impression intensifies when we take into account the depressed economic state of Maine's interior— lots of trailers and deteriorating homes, and beat-up sedans driven by men in white T-shirts and baseball caps, with long razor-cut sideburns. Once we pass two men raking hay by hand. This somehow strikes me as a luxury—how do they have time to do that? I guess our bicycling must provoke a similar reaction in some people, but we feel right in synch with these old-fashioned farmers. They wave.

Saw two good names today in the our first big Maine town, Fryeburg: Maine's US Rep. Olympia J. Snowe; and a kid in North Covell's swim program, on a list posted in a store window: Django Bliss.

I notice the first instance of Down East talk, from a corner grocer: "What ah ya lookin' fah?" A fellow in the same store, obviously from Boston or thereabouts, made "that" into two syllables—"thee-at." Then this call-and-response between the clerk and a customer:

> "It's good for Maine."
> "It's good for everybody."

Lakes, called "ponds" hereabouts, are becoming more and more frequent. There's a big one at South Paris, near where we provision ourselves while black clouds gather in the west. The store is in Norway, just past Sweden, and other nearby towns are called Poland, Egypt, Warsaw, and Moscow. From here it's five miles to the top of Streaked Mountain, an 800-foot climb followed by a descent of equal length into Buckfield. The wind whips the birches, and blows curtains of dirt from bare lots, sandblasting me and my bike.

In Buckfield rough-looking men holler at us from the doors of taverns, but we're more worried by the approaching storm, and eager to camp before it hits. Martin Stream Campground is three more miles on pavement, followed by a short descent into the woods on a dirt road. Our hosts turn out to be a friendly couple with heavy Down East accents. We choose a site under a thick low growth of pines, well-sheltered.

In spite, or because, of our haste in pitching our tents, the storm misses us. Elsewhere, we heard later, it dropped several inches of rain. We eat our sauteed veggies and rice in peace, except for a few mosquitoes. A couple next door in an RV donates half of a watermelon, perfectly ripe. They're from Williamsport, Pennsylvania, and had originally intended to camp in a more remote site about 60 miles north, which turned out to be dominated by an Outward Bound group, one of whom had "flipped his lid" and was being sat on by others till the sheriff arrived. So these folks had excess food, much of which we inherited.

June 30th Day 75
67 miles
Turner — Damariscotta, Maine

Next morning it's sunny but windy, blowing steadily from the northwest. Our starts have become even later since the Ramseys signed on—today we're riding by 11:30. The espresso pot might have something to do with it.

Also, it's slightly unnerving with Chris along. Nanci and I are used to our own conservative riding styles, steady and cautious. Now here's the 14 year-old boy, spurting ahead then coasting, swerving, skidding to stops, then falling behind on hills. And, like Missouri, Maine has some hills—short but steep and plentiful.

I also thought of New Jersey at one point, particularly the Pine Barrens, with its sandy soil, scrub pines, and proximity to the sea; and the dilapidated groceries, rusty old wrecks, and trailer dwellings. Famished, we stop for pizza at one building, set back in the trees a little ways and looking very temporary. An enormous fat woman and a muscular dark-haired man in a white undershirt with tattooed arms serve us frozen pizza, and we help ourselves to soda from the reach-in. Outside they're logging birches with earth-moving machinery, bulldozing the skinny trees, turning up the brush, and leaving only piles of dirt blowing in the wind. Maine, I'm told, produces 100 million toothpicks every working day.

Out of Dresden Mills we crest Blinn Hill and are granted a panoramic view of the country. It's a beautiful clear afternoon and in every direction spread low, rolling, forested hills, and beyond them to the west and north hazy blue mountains. One particularly large peak could have been either Mt. Washington or perhaps Mt. Katadin, Maine's tallest.

Down the other side of the hill the country is opening up—I'm eagerly looking for signs of the sea—when suddenly a car comes up behind us, honking its horn. It's none other than Alden Rust Kent, schoolboy friend and newly-repatriated Mainiac, who has been hunting us on back roads for five hours, thanks to some messages and sketchy routes I left on his answering machine. We promptly dump our packs in his car and he goes ahead down the road as we race along, light and free, past someplace called Cowshit Corner, toward Damariscotta.

Passing Damariscotta Mills, where the huge turreted Kavanaugh House looks over a pond from a hilltop, a man, with his wife and kids in the car, slows, rolls down his window, and hollers something about a bald eagle in a treetop a quarter-mile back by the Damariscotta River. Soon we've all gathered to admire the majestic bird, arrogantly surveying the surrounding woods and water from his bare perch.

Alden had told us that the wealthy and fashionable vacationers, "people from away" (anyone whose parents weren't born in Maine), have pushed the resentful natives further and further back into the woods by driving up property values, first along the coast, then along the ponds and rivers. There are some fine homes along our route as we descend toward the sea, most of them painted white and many dating from the 19th century.

Damariscotta still holds on to some of the cosmopolitan charm of its seafaring past. The business district is a narrow street along which tall brick buildings march up a slight incline. Fishing and pleasure boats crowd the river. Artsy-craftsy signs are everywhere, announcing antiques for sale, restaurants, gifts, or just tourist information. Further on, up some more hills (naturally) and down them (law of gravity) is our campground by Lake Pemaquid, which is actually a river. We pick a site, lock our bikes to a tree, and then Alden drives us down to his boyhood stomping ground, Christmas Cove on Rutherford Island. We drive out the long narrow peninsula between the Pemaquid and Damariscotta Rivers, developing en route a fine Portland Lager euphoria. We actually wouldn't have known we were on a peninsula if Alden hadn't told us so, nor would we have necessarily realized we were crossing over to an island on the tiny drawbridge. But out at the end of the road, we can clamber down a sandy bank to stand on some rocks in the salty shallows, gazing out at the further islands, multi-colored lobster buoys brilliant in the setting sun. The Atlantic Ocean at last, though we still have a few more days to our final destination.

Captain John Brown first made landfall here in 1625. Then as now, white granite shelved into the calm sea, somewhat protected by a chain of pine-dotted rocky islands offshore. Today brightly colored lobster buoys dot the calm salt water. Although bigger crustaceans can be taken offshore, in deeper water, 70% of them are caught inshore—it's easier, for one thing. Supposedly there are 40-pounders crawling around on the bottom out there a thousand feet down.

Lobstering is very regulated here—you don't just go casually laying out a wire trap or a netted oak-slat trap. The State of Maine licenses the lobstermen (lobsterpeople?), who then need to find a place to lay out their traps. The best places, needless to say, are taken, and passed down through generations. But the soaring value of seafront real estate is reducing the number of available docks for lobster smacks.

We dine at the venerable Coveside restaurant on Christmas Cove, where Alden hears from Hannah, our young waitress, about babysitting for his cousins the Rusts, who live in the house he summered in and with whom his branch of the family is no longer intimate.

Unfortunately, the Coveside is out of lobster, so we order other, less regional dishes. They won't take a credit card, but they do let me write my name and address on the back of the check, so a bill can be sent. Like many such establishments in similar seasonal resorts (it's quiet as the grave here in the winter) the Coveside has changed hands nearly every year, or burned down, but allowing cash-poor customers to sign for the check without previous arrangements (or any identification, for that matter) is one tradition that's persisted for a long time. Hannah says they've only gotten stiffed once.

July 1st   Day 76
49.4 miles
Damariscotta — Lincolnville Beach, Maine

A cool, dry night and then the morning brings brilliant sun. From our elevated campsite we can see, through the trees and over the roofs of a few RVs, the glimmering river.

After some coffee and baked goods from the camp store, we're off at about 10:30. Ramsey's been having derailleur trouble, which we cannot remedy, so he's confined to a few gears. The next bike shop is in Camden.

Route 1 North is busy, but along this stretch the shoulder is good and wide. Still following our mapped route, we leave the highway and plummet into Waldeboro, another narrow brick town, then climb out again and regain Route 1. An inland shortcut on 90 takes us to Rockport/Camden, where a kindly local nurse (male) gives us directions to avoid traffic and get on the scenic route around Rockport to Camden.

The nurse has accosted us outside a great little gourmet market, with exotic foods, tremendous selection of beers and wines, and complimentary premium coffee to sip while we shop. Our kind of place.

Entering Rockport we ride by rows of stately old white houses. Our scenic route takes us along shady lanes, past a herd of Belted Galloway cows—black with a broad white band around their middle and a cute, snubbed, terrier-like face—and glimpses of a beautiful harbor set into the hills, cradling clusters of masts.

Camden is total two-way gridlock between rows of boutiques and cafes, and narrow sidewalks crowded with the usual strange tourist and local types. Some of us patronize the Ben & Jerry's ice cream store while Ramsey discovers that the bike shop doesn't have the derailleur he needs, which they had told him over the phone was available.

Our road out of Camden follows the base of a hill, past a small ski area, then hugs the shore of a pond before climbing to Lincolnville Center. I called the campsite we'd selected, near Searsport, but it turned out they had recently implemented a restrictive policy of one week's minimum stay. So we aborted our Route 1 bypass and descended to the sea once again.

We hit the coast at Lincolnville Beach. Still a beautiful day, with golden light from the west and the briny iodine smell of the seashore. It's actually the first time we've attained a view of the Atlantic under our own steam. We regrouped and rested for a few minutes at a public park next to the water, where there was a lobster pound—a local sort of establishment, usually a whitewashed shack next to a large raised tub of live lobsters. The feisty beasts have thick rubber bands around their claws, or small wooden pegs driven into the base of these fearsome pincers. For the going market price—currently $7.95-9.95—they will pluck one from the tank and boil it for you in about 15-20 minutes.

We continued riding a few miles north to the Old Massachusetts Homestead Campground, which offered sites deep in the trees at the base of a big ridge. Plenty of mosquitoes and even a critter, a bulky little coon I spotted in my headlamp beam on the way to the washroom. The next morning some of the contents of one of my packs were scattered on the ground.

It would be easier, though less adventurous, if campgrounds and motels were named to accurately reflect their features. We'd have the Tiny Towel Motel, Barking Dog Campground, Road Noise Inn, or Mosquito Pond Resort. Some of the humbler stores and restaurants along our way have adopted the strategy of dispensing with names altogether; rather than an ornament, their name is what they offer: BEER ICE SODA or PIZZA BREAKFAST 6 A.M. Motels will be the last holdout in this new era of minimalist roadside service; I find it hard to imagine romance at the B&W TV COFFEE or at the $32 DOUBLE.

July 2nd Day 77
46.5 miles
Lincolnville Beach — Ellsworth, Maine

Cloudy today, and by the time we were packed up, breakfasted and turning back on to Route 1, it began to rain.

Riding with Ramsey and Christopher was a little difficult yesterday—I

---

would have liked to take advantage of the good weather to ride beyond Searsport to the next campground; Nanci and I could have made the distance well before dark, but our two friends were unwilling to ride what would have totalled 60-65 miles. I can't blame them, remembering what we felt like after that first day, climbing Mt. Palomar.

But it's been just the two of us for thousands of miles, and sometimes, climbing a hill in my ruminative, low-gear mentality, I feel we've lost control of our ride here at its conclusion. Maybe our ride really ended at Ticonderoga, or even in the Adirondacks, and these last ten days are just the winding down from it. Our private experience across 4500 miles of America, shared with good friends at the start, has now become public again at the end. Well then, I think, speeding down the other side of the hill in my singsong high-gear euphoria, the company's worth it. And Ramsey *does* have this espresso pot . . .

Terrain along the coast is hilly. Out in the harbors and inlets the islands sit high on their rocky bases, shaggy pines elevated above the smooth water as if on a table. Crystalline white granite shelves down into the shallows, as if the Desolation Wilderness or similar High Sierra ground were folded over to meet a quiet Pacific bay.

We keep groping for other states to compare Maine with: the interior, from Fryeburg to Lewiston, sometimes looked like the Jersey Pine Barrens, with the scraped raw earth, pine-lined secondary roads, junked cars and nameless shacks serving greasy food. To Nanci the birches, short spruces, and frequent cloudiness resembled Alaska. As before, we often thought of Missouri, and nearer the coast, the lakes with high pine-spiked ridges in the background reminded me of Tahoe.

So we're riding in the rain again, most of the time on a nice wide shoulder. Traffic on Route 1 is definitely getting heavier. Ten miles north is Belfast, where we divert to the coast from the highway and go into Barbara's for breakfast. In spite of looking like a bus stop, Barbara's offers buckwheat pancakes and well-chilled fresh orange juice. Karen is expected to drive out from Vermont today, so Ramsey makes certain to always park his bike in a conspicuous place every time we stop, and hang his yellow helmet from a handlebar.

Outside it continues to rain, and after another ten miles we're all pretty soaked by the time we cross the big bridges at Bucksport. Even our technologically-advanced GoreTex raingear is thoroughly wet, inside and out.

East Orland comes up nearly ten miles later, and on the left is a little grocery that has a six-stool snack bar. It's dry inside, and passably warm, and in its aisles between racks of canned goods and videotapes we change our wet inner layers for dry ones, then sit on our dripping outerwear and feast on chili, pizza, hot tea and ice cream as fast as the two young women can serve us.

A guy comes along with a bike rack on his car and says he'll give us a ride to Ellsworth, the next big town. Ramsey and Chris accept the offer, but Nanci and I, with true dedication, ride ten or eleven more miles north until we see a yellow helmet outside a door at the Twilite Motel. Soon we're in our own room with every single bag and article of clothing spread out to dry, all the heaters blasting. It's the wettest we've ever been on this trip.

Later in the evening Karen shows up in her orange Volvo, having driven seven hours from Rochester through the rain. She drives us all first to a "laundry-mat," to use the dryers, then to a Holiday Inn restaurant (Oliver's, named after Oliver Ellsworth, America's "forgotten founding father" and an early Supreme Court justice) because it's the only thing open after 9 p.m.

July 3rd, 1986   Day 78
29.7 miles
Ellsworth — Bar Harbor, Maine
Total mileage on odometer: 4657.7

Move with the sense of having arrived every step of the way.
—Edward Espe Brown

The past 77 days have been remarkable in that they've been filled with arrivals: a new state line, the motel or campground at the end of the day, a little cafe for lunch or snacks, even the top of the next hill. And we never consulted a US map—just larger-scale route maps. Even the

AAA state maps we used showed a definite couple of inches of progress each day. We've divided the past three months of our lives into these little destinations, and each one has given its share of satisfaction.

Dick, the manager/owner of the Twilite Motel here in Ellsworth, is very enthusiastic about our trip. We should have hired him as our promoter. Last night he buttonholed tired travelers as they checked in, telling them about our adventure. "Sure buddy, just gimme a room." Early this morning he knocked on our door, calling out, "Hey, you've hit the big time, the newspaper's here!" Dick has called the *Ellsworth American,* published by James Russell Wiggins, 83-year-old former *Washington Post* executive editor and LBJ's UN ambassador. When it was founded in 1850, the Ellsworth paper's slogan was "Americans can govern America without the help of foppish influence."

Wiggins has sent over Tom Field, a nice young reporter, to interview us for 45 minutes in our room, which is hung with damp smelly socks and underwear. Dick is pretty hyped-up; he asked Tom to take our picture for the article in front of the motel sign.

Since the skies are still threatening, Ramsey and Chris have decided to drive with Karen to Bar Harbor, but they all meet us for breakfast at Dick's (no relation to our host of last night), in an old corner building in this bustling town of 5000 (same population as in 1850). Billed by our reporter as a greasy spoon, Dick's is actually okay. Good pancakes, and the cook keeps hollering questions over his range about our trip. According to him, we're not going far enough. We need to ride to Eastport, about 100 miles north, to attain the easternmost point on the coast. Of course, I didn't point out to him that we didn't start at the westernmost, nor even the southernmost point on the other coast. Aesthetically, Bar Harbor and Oceanside seem to be a good match.

Happily, our route out of Ellsworth deviates from the very crowded Route 1. We ride south to Owl's Point, and around to meet the bridge to Mt. Desert Island. For the last time on this trip, like we did so many times in the Midwest, we ride side-by-side down the middle of a rural road with very little traffic. When we reach Route 1, with a sudden explosion of lobster joints, antique barns, and holiday traffic, we pick up a bike lane for the rest of the way.

The rain is confined to an occasional light drizzle. Ahead, the island's mountains, dominated by Cadillac Mountain looming 1000 feet above the sea, hunch over so their heads don't scratch the low sky. We ride up and down steep little hills taking in harbor views from every direction. Ahead is Northeast Harbor, with big homes and a heritage of part-time residents like the Rockefellers, Kennedys, and their ilk. We turn north instead and roll downhill under an old stone bridge into the traffic-jammed, trendy, colorful narrow streets of Bar Harbor.

Two bicycles roll to the end of the pier, ferryboats and lobster smacks anchored on smooth gray water beneath a gray sky. We walk down a concrete ramp to the sea, where salt water washes over my shoes. The journey has been its own end, every day a complete voyage. Today offers no special reason to rejoice or regret. It's just another arrival.

Ramsey and the gang showed up with a bottle of champagne, after which we tore down the gear, loaded it on Alden and Diane's Jeep, and drove to the first lobster pound. Definitely fresh stuff—boiled up right before our eyes. As they say around these parts, "Wicked good!"

A few days later, as we hurtle home in a pressurized cabin at 600 mph, I look down at a distant, shrunken America and remember how our bicycles held us so close to all the smells, sights, tastes and feelings along the way. Now we're crossing the Mississippi at 35,000 feet, and I see Henry Harris, Peter, and the father of the high school bicycle racer in Missouri, trying to wave us down.

Afterword

Allons! The road is before us!
It is safe—I have tried it—my own feet have tried it
      well—be not detain'd!
Let the paper remain on the desk unwritten, and the
      book on the shelf unopen'd!
Let the tools remain in the workshop! let the money
      remain unearn'd!
Let the school stand! mind not the cry of the teacher!
Let the preacher preach in his pulpit! let the lawyer
      plead in the court, and the judge
         expound the law.
Camerado, I give you my hand!
I give you my love more precious than money;
I give you myself before preaching or law;
Will you give me yourself? will you come travel with
      me?
Shall we stick by each other as long as we live?

—*Walt Whitman*